equal measure, intrigue, and even suspense. It will astound and thrill anyone, surely inspiring some to read or reread well-known works by the great French romantic writer."

—**Tom Conner**
Professor of Modern Languages
and Literatures, St. Norbert College, and author of
Chateaubriand's Mémoires d'outre-tombe: Portrait of an Artist in Exile

"By presenting an absorbing arc of ancestry, Daniel Fallon reveals a side of Chateaubriand too little recognized, yet as instructive to students of the influential French romantic writer, politician, and diplomat as it is compelling to today's reader of biography."

—**Steven Mansbach**
Distinguished University Professor and Professor of Art
History and Archaeology, University of Maryland at College Park

Love's Legacy

Love's Legacy

Viscount Chateaubriand *and the* Irish Girl

DANIEL FALLON

Santa Fe, New Mexico

Published by: Amazonas Publishing
    PO Box 32988
    Santa Fe, NM 87594-2988
    www.amazonaspublishing.com

Editors: Ann Mason, Ellen Kleiner
Book design and production: Janice St. Marie
Cover art: Elena Lacey

FIRST EDITION

Printed in Canada

Publisher's Cataloging-in-Publication Data
Names: Fallon, Daniel, 1938- author. | Gillespie, Gerald, 1933- writer of
    foreword.
Title: Love's legacy : Viscount Chateaubriand and the Irish girl / Daniel
    Fallon ; foreword by Gerald Gillespie.
Description: First edition. | Santa Fe, New Mexico : Amazonas Publishing,
    [2021]
Identifiers: ISBN: 9781735999609 (hardcover) | 9781735999623 (paper-
    back) | 9781735999616 (ebook) | LCCN: 2020920765
Subjects: LCSH: Chateaubriand, François-René, vicomte de,
    1768-1848--Exile--England. | Chateaubriand, François-René,
    vicomte de, 1768-1848--Relations with women. | Chateaubriand,
    François-René, vicomte de, 1768-1848--Children.. | Authors,
    French--19th century--Biography. | Fallon, Mary Neale, approx-
    imately 1780-approximately 1826-- Children. | Fallon, Thomas,
    approximately 1800-1863--Family. | Fallon family--Genealogy. |
    Colombia--Biography.

Classification: LCC: PQ2205.Z5 F35 2021 | DDC: 848/.609--dc23

1 3 5 7 9 10 8 6 4 2

For Mary

Acknowledgments

Many persons have taken interest in the work laid out in this book, assisted in the collection of documents and other artifacts, and encouraged avenues of inquiry and interpretation. I owe special thanks to Pierre Riberette (1929–2010) and George D. Painter (1914–2005), foremost scholars of the life and works of Chateaubriand. They were especially stimulated by the early findings and continually lent support, often providing me their analyses and sending me their own supplemental research.

The indefatigable intelligent efforts of my genealogist in London, Edward J. Lowe, were invaluable. Isabel Neuschwander, the enterprising and resourceful director of archives for the Département de la Somme, in Amiens, responded with alacrity to my entreaties. She searched determinedly with her colleagues and ultimately turned up revelatory documents unknown to the world of Chateaubriand scholarship. She, her staff, and her successor, François Giustiniani, deserve due credit for their contribution, along with my humble thanks.

Of the several *chateaubriandistes* who engaged me, one couple stands out. I owe a special debt to the kindness and personal care of Professor Jacques Gury and his wife, Odile. They guided me and my wife through several homes in the countryside of Brittany where Chateaubriand spent time in his youth, fed us galettes for which the Bretons are famous, and accompanied us to Mass in the Saint-Malo Cathedral. Through his continuous correspondence, Professor Gury ensured that I was never far from Chateaubriand and his Breton roots.

I thank Carolyn Gates and Jean-Philippe Gury for their assistance in providing translations of essays and materials from French to English for my study. I have also benefited, as will the reader, from critiques and editorial recommendations by specialists familiar with Chateaubriand scholarship, as well as other scholars and editors. Among those who each provided a careful review of early drafts of the full manuscript are Maureen Allen, Tom Conner, Gerald Gillespie, June Hargrove, Axel Markert, Ann Mason, Virgil Nemoianu, Elihu Pearlman, and Amy Schwartz. My uncle Donn R. Byrne, younger brother of my mother, prodded me incessantly to bring this project to completion. My sister, Pat Fallon, a painter and printmaker who shares my genetic proximity to the Irish girl, read drafts of the manuscript carefully, providing encouragement and insightful suggestions.

Finally, I owe my patient wife and daughters, Chris, Katy, and Sylvia, an expression of deep appreciation. They have lived with this tale in many forms, can recite parts of it to any willing audience, tolerated my obsession with humor and grace, and sustained my energy by reflecting my love and admiration for them.

Contents

Foreword

Dr. Daniel Fallon is so well known nationally and internationally as a top US-based academician and adviser on education and cultural programs that it may surprise some readers to encounter him here as the teller of a family legend stretching over many generations. From the start, we find ourselves in the grip of an unfolding great story, one rooted both in the glamorous heyday of European romanticism and in the adventurous opening of the New World nation of Colombia, Fallon's own birthplace. The autobiographical narrator, who speaks also as a serious historian, almost faces the necessity to split himself into multiple personalities as he simultaneously pursues inquiries into French literature and his own ancestry to discover the secrets of his family's legacy. In Fallon's account, a kind of timeless romantic fairy tale competes with history until, ultimately, they merge in a higher synthesis.

This reviewer is only one of a number of people in several countries who at intervals have enjoyed earlier glimpses into Fallon's historical research. Over recent decades, with archival zeal and earnest exploration of pertinent sites, the modern savant Fallon has plumbed the life and writings of Chateaubriand and likewise the patterns and records pertaining to the viscount's possible son, Thomas Fallon—Daniel Fallon's great-great-grandfather—born to Mary Fallon in London around 1800. And there is, as crucial further background, the distinguished history of the Fallon family for two centuries in Colombia, with their multifarious achievements in the arts and sciences as well as political life. Thus, *Love's Legacy* bears a rough analogy to an iceberg, most of which, the assiduous research pursued over decades, rides invisible under water supporting the brilliant top—the book's concluding revelations.

Present-day readers are privileged to follow Daniel Fallon, inheritor of this saga, as he articulates the many stages of discovery and analysis. Among other things, assuming the role of a supernarrator, our investigator narrator retrospectively interprets an earlier major author's challenging practice of "occultation" (a useful term borrowed here from research into pre-Enlightenment, especially mannerist, painting and literature). If Chateaubriand happens to be observing from somewhere in an afterlife, he surely must be pleased by the effort Fallon has made to decipher for today's readers key instances in the viscount's own famous autobiographical writings where he apparently transposes the identities of lovers to protect both his own social status and the welfare of others in the less-tolerant world of his times.

Central among vexing puzzles is whether, during the political restoration in France, an already married and prominent Chateaubriand took pains to foster the elite education of the youthful Thomas Fallon only out of love for the boy's Irish mother and gratitude for her assistance during his days of penurious exile in Britain or because he actually was Thomas's father. An open admission of paternity by Chateaubriand would have unleashed harsh laws in both France and Britain and would have wrecked the families involved. As Thomas's descendant, Daniel Fallon has at his disposal to solve this mystery the additional instruments of modern science nonexistent in the revolutionary era. In later stages of his quest, Daniel Fallon meticulously pursues scientific avenues in keeping with today's standards to determine any biological link to Chateaubriand. The pursuit of forensic research of several kinds lends the narrative one of the prime qualities of detective fiction (incidentally, a genre largely spawned in the romantic era). As a humanist loyal to the modern scientific approach, Daniel Fallon does not hedge his findings. After they have been passed through the filter of science, the final gathering of the several evidentiary threads adds zest to the book's close.

Today's readers will gain historical perspective as they ponder the modern narrator's analysis of who presumed what in the early nineteenth century and as he weighs this legacy against the accrued information from his vigorous new searching. The quest for answers is the motor force. But something else of great worth emerges quietly and convincingly in the picture the narrator portrays of his own father, Carlos. In references to him, the family romance seems recapitulated more expansively with its own special traits. After glamorous youthful adventure to China, Carlos effectively changed nations through the act of settling in New Orleans, where his father was serving as consul general of Colombia, and, as Daniel Fallon's family research shows, he evolved into a (North) American who evinced traits of an irrepressible polymath. Something of the extraterritorial roaming and widely branching inquisitiveness of Chateaubriand and Thomas Fallon seems to have blossomed again later in Carlos, on whom his son casts a fond and appreciative eye.

Daniel Fallon gives us a very personal book, a both fascinating and factually specific account that exhibits at the same time something archetypal: the risk-taking spirit in the unfolding of the larger human story.

—**Gerald Gillespie**
Professor Emeritus of Comparative Literature and
Professor Emeritus of German Studies,
Stanford University

Preface

The research behind the narrative in the following pages began in 1989 when I inherited two letters written in 1817 to my great-great-grandfather, Thomas Fallon. One was signed by the famous nineteenth-century writer François-René de Chateaubriand and the other conveyed his permissions and was signed by his secretary. I knew that Chateaubriand was widely regarded as the founder of modern French literature, having directly influenced generations of French literary figures who followed him, creating a uniquely French aesthetic. Why had the esteemed writer, flamboyant diplomat, and audacious autobiographer dictated an affectionate note to my great-great-grandfather? What was the relationship between them? How did their lives intersect? These letters demanded answers from me, a scholar working among scholars, and launched me on a quest of discovery.

Early findings from my quest led to an invitation to present my work in preliminary form in the *Bulletin de la Société Chateaubriand* in 1996.[1] I subsequently delivered invited lectures in Brittany during the sesquicentennial anniversary of the death of François-René de Chateaubriand in 1998, first at an event organized by the US Consulate in Rennes and later in Saint-Malo for the Société Chateaubriand.[2] My research continued well beyond this time, competing with the demands of unrelated full-time employment. Ultimately, the accumulated evidence resulting from my discoveries came into focus as a coherent tale that is the subject of this book.

A description of the colorful events in Saint-Malo on the 150th anniversary of Chateaubriand's death, July 4, 1998, offers a fitting prelude to the story I relate here. I experienced directly how this somber celebration underscored Chateaubriand's stature as a revered figure who had greatly impacted French literary tradition and inspired many by his adventurous spirit and range of roles in life. The ceremony began with a pilgrimage to the Grand Bé, the tiny uninhabited island just beyond the shore of Saint-Malo that is home to Chateaubriand's solitary grave, a setting reflecting his love of the sea. To take advantage of low tide, which enables pedestrian access, the procession began at 9:45 a.m. At the grave-side, the assembly, numbering hundreds, sang "La Marseillaise" in preparation for speeches from the deputy mayor of Saint-Malo, René Couanau; the renowned editor of Chateaubriand's works and president of the Société Chateaubriand, Pierre Riber-ette; and, finally, an emissary from the Vatican's pontifical council for culture, Cardinal Paul Poupard. An honor guard of French cadets, as well as a contingent in eighteenth-century Republican Guard uniforms, stood at parade rest throughout the event. A choir of Breton fishermen, in denim sailing clothes, sang seafaring songs, accompanying themselves with traditional Breton folk instruments. The local high school band played somber funeral music. Others observed the festivities from the sea in boats. The sky was overcast and gloomy, just as Chateaubriand would have liked it, given his penchant for melancholy.

The following morning, a Sunday, occasioned a grand celebra-tory Mass in the Saint-Malo Cathedral, befitting an author who had written an influential book on Christianity. The Mass began with a procession of twenty knights of the Order of the Maltese Cross—a society that had once initiated Chateaubriand—wear-ing white robes emblazoned with large black crosses. Organ music swelled full-throated from the large pipes, while the smaller pipes produced sounds resembling a chorus of trumpets. An altar boy swinging an incense-packed thurible was so inspired that the sanc-tuary swiftly filled with perfumed smoky vapor, challenging noses and eyes. The cardinal officiated in the presence of priests from sixteen local parishes, who assisted in the ritual blessing of the sacrament. A stirring choir sang intermittently. It was the kind of high religious spectacle that would have thrilled Chateaubriand. My host, Professor Jacques Gury, whispered to me that no other French writer could command this kind of ecclesiastical respect. Chateaubriand had been a Catholic and a sinner, he explained, and had managed each role with aplomb and finesse, an apt commentary on a writer who had both extolled the artistry of Catholic Church ritual and lived a flamboyant lifestyle unconstrained by Church-condoned behavior.

Love's Legacy focuses on aspects of Chateaubriand's life, character, and literary intelligence in the context of the times and customs in which he and his contemporaries lived, leading to an adventure as I sought to resolve a genealogical mystery related to my own ancestors. Since many of the sources that bring this chronicle to life are recorded only in French, translation presents a special challenge. Words, which convey meaning, are important guideposts to understanding in a historical hunt for clues to a puzzle. Therefore, I give English translations as I lay out the research, but to allow readers of French to confirm fidelity of meaning I have provided notes containing the French originals in important instances. In some cases, I have benefited from recent English translations in the public domain,[3] but even then I have occasionally interpolated meanings based on my own understanding. This exciting venture of both professional and personal exploration brought me closer to French civilization than I had ever anticipated. It has been a rich and fulfilling journey.

—**Daniel Fallon**
Santa Fe, New Mexico
March 2021

CHAPTER 1

Taking the Baton
to Begin the Quest

GENERATIONS PERSIST.

With an ending, it began. "He's gone," my mother said simply when I answered the telephone. I was soon flying to her side, following the death of my father, to comfort her and help with final arrangements. When I arrived, I discovered that she had already organized the funeral, with some details fittingly unusual. My father Carlos had throughout his life been an entertaining storyteller, using his ingenious imagination, rich knowledge, and natural sense of wonder to comprehend the world in which he found himself. Most of his stories, like Chateaubriand's, were anchored in his own life and informed by his unique perspective, yet linked to more universal human experience.

My father had also been afflicted all his adult life with what he called "a religious hang-up," resulting in virtuous rebellion against the agents of Church authority on the one hand and irksome submission to deep religious feelings on the other. Raised a Catholic in Bogotá, Colombia, Carlos had left the Church angrily after being forbidden to read Darwin. As he had explained to me later, he had gone out on his own, tracked God down, and had a productive conversation. God had told him that as long as he led a moral life and tried to avoid hurting other people he could read Darwin or, for that matter, any book he wanted.

Carlos's complicated feelings about religion had inspired him to familiarize himself with as many world religions as he could. This aspiration could have partly reflected a desire to keep some measure of belief in magic, but he had also reasoned that the worst calamity would be to die, go to some afterlife, and find the wrong god in charge of the place. Available evidence and his practical logic had led him to conclude that the odds of an afterlife were diminishingly small. Nonetheless, given the constraints of contemporaneous knowledge, he could not reduce the probability to zero. That meant, by his calculation, it would be prudent to prepare for an afterlife just in case. Further reasoning convinced him that the best protection was to believe in all plausible gods simultaneously, with equal fervor. His motivation was so strong that it prompted him to learn ancient Sumerian, Greek, Hebrew, and Latin, so he could study original religious texts on his own. In this respect he mirrored Chateaubriand, whose study of Christianity was enhanced by his familiarity with age-old languages.

Carlos had made good progress in assimilating religious teachings of indigenous peoples in the far reaches of the Upper Amazon, where he had spent his early career as an officer in the Colombian Navy, and of other societies, especially teachings relayed by seafarers of the Pacific Ocean. As an adolescent held prisoner in northern China for eighteen months, for example, he explored Chinese religious beliefs. He also found ancient Egyptian religious teachings persuasive, understanding them better than many scholars.

My sister and I were not raised as Catholics. After we moved to Washington, DC, however, when we were seven and eight, respectively, my mother insisted that we go to church on Sundays so we could understand what religion in the United States was all about. My father's solution was to take us to a different church each Sunday until he found one that satisfied his criteria: the sermons had to be thoughtful, scholarly, and interesting; and the congregation had to read books. We ended up joining the First Congregational Church of Washington, DC.

When, late in life, Carlos retired to the coast of North Carolina, he found himself surrounded by Southern Baptists and unclassifiable evangelicals. He chose to exercise his fine sense of dialectic in this environment by reverting to Catholicism. He liked the way it was viewed by most local inhabitants as a sinister cult embraced by weak-minded sinners with suspicious ties to foreigners. Carlos explained to me that he had actually never left the Church but had gone on sabbatical to allow it time to mature. In the meantime, the Church had obliged by modifying its teachings and permitting worshippers to read books, including Darwin. Carlos's sudden discovery of the value of Catholic ritual, provoked by a change in his life circumstances, was much like the abrupt conversion Chateaubriand experienced, causing the French writer to extol the Church in his famous treatise *The Genius of Christianity.*

Following Carlos's death, my mother arranged with the little Catholic church in Southport, North Carolina, for a funeral. Informed by deep knowledge of my father, however, she understood that he would not want to take chances with the afterlife.

Since he had taught her that many religions required a deceased person to arrive in the netherworld intact, she would not let his body be embalmed. To meet local health codes, she therefore had the funeral conducted within seventy-two hours of his death. Before the coffin was closed, she carefully placed inside it a package containing a silver dollar—for him to give the boatman when crossing the river to the other side—and provisions for the trip, including tins of sardines, some rye crisps, and a compass.

The clouds that had accompanied his death gave way to sunshine on the bright morning of my father's funeral. My mother was the first to notice the solitary gull circling overhead before it glided down toward us as the casket was being blessed for lowering into the sandy coastal soil. "It is a salute," she said softly, taking my hand as the bird flew off toward the sea. Pressing her hand, I thought silently, "What else could it be?"—allowing the supernatural world, whose presence my father had nurtured within me, to flow once more into the rational, habitual, temporal domain of my everyday life.

Seeing the gull supplanted my sorrowful emptiness with hope and confidence, the bird's dependence on the sea linking it to that vast water world covering more than seventy percent of the earth's surface, as old as the planet itself, symbolizing eternity— an enticement of fascination and wonder for every generation of humankind. Carlos, for instance, had loved the sea, becoming a sailor at age fourteen and later, as a young man, commander in chief of the Colombian Navy before immigrating with us to the United States late in 1940, when I was two years old. During World War II, he had enlisted in the US armed forces, acquired US citizenship, and risen quickly to the rank of captain in what was then the Army Air Corps. After 1945, he had supported our family as a lecturer and writer before teaching himself, through self-organized study at the Library of Congress, what was needed to acquire a license as an engineer, an orderly profession that satisfied the aspects of his inexhaustible intellect related to science, mathematics, and design. Within five years of starting as an engineer at a local firm, Carlos had advanced to corporate staff of RCA Corporation, having established a new branch of engineering.[1] When his earning years had trailed off, he had chosen to retire by the sea, that comforting expanse on which he had discovered an independent life away from the home of his parents.

After the burial, we returned to the house to receive friends and other guests. When everyone had left and my mother was resting, I went to my father's study. On the desk in front of me lay the memorial service program. The cover read simply: "Carlos Fallon, January 21, 1909–February 12, 1989." Nearby were his file cabinets, containing the records he wanted me to have. I opened a drawer labeled Family and removed several manila folders. Suddenly I remembered from some distant past an observation made by a friend: "The death of a parent is always devastating." Since my father's death had been both natural and expected, I had not felt the loss with much force until now, with these files about our family in hand. As I began to sort through the folders, which his fingers had so often and so carefully touched, with heightened awareness I realized that he was no longer a resource to answer any lingering questions I might have about the contents of the files or the fascinating tales he wove from them. When he and I had sat together in his study, the files had often been the launching point for some fabulous tale sprung from our ancestry. Never had I felt the need for interpretation, because my father was a gifted storyteller, whose voice immediately drew my attention away from the documents and into a Technicolor world of people from another time experiencing life as they found it, with all its compelling twists and turns.

As I delved into the files, they began to conjure titillating unfinished business. My father had carefully protected the old documents, endowing them with the mystery one feels in stories about treasure maps or hidden codes. He had not kept them away from me or treated them as secrets. He had simply stored them, perhaps for his own further study or for me or others to explore. Just as we cannot expect a child to remember the moment of first recognizing a parent, I cannot recall first becoming aware of the papers. In my mind they were always there. Now that they were mine, however, I felt a pressing need to understand them. Only later would I learn that with this gift my dying father was handing me a repository of love, launching me on a mission of discovery.

Suddenly, disturbing my reverie, four white envelopes fell from a folder in my hands to the floor. As I picked them up I noticed, displayed on the front of one envelope in the less-secure handwriting reflective of my father's old age and recent illness, a message written in pencil: "These envelopes (4) contain the letters from Hyacinthe Pilorge (Chateaubriand's secretary) to young Thomas Fallon about his education. They are all falling apart and have to be pieced together—the dates may be important."

Inside the envelopes were the remains of a smaller envelope and two old letters turned brown and brittle by the chemistry of air with paper over the nearly two centuries since they had been written. The paper had broken into numerous small stiff pieces, but I could see the writing, in French, on several of them. One piece revealed the dramatic flourish of a signature that seemed to form the letters *Ch*, suggesting to me a relic of the presence of Chateaubriand, who had figured prominently in our family lore.

I knew that among my father's magical family stories, one was about an Irish girl named Mary O'Neill and the famous French writer and diplomat François-René de Chateaubriand. When Carlos lowered his voice to invoke the past, I, along with other listeners, traveled with him to whatever time and place he beckoned forth. We were drawn into a world of people long gone yet alive in the tale unfolding before us. I suppose, like any child in the presence of a talented storyteller, I would sit quietly while Carlos invoked his magic, never feeling a need to memorize the filigree of details that sustained the rapture of each moment. In my mind the narratives occupied a universe belonging to Carlos. I imagined he would always be there to tell them again.

Now, with these extraordinary old documents in front of me, I struggled to remember what my father had said about them. Fortunately, he had committed some of the story to writing. When he was forty years old, he had completed an engaging autobiography in his characteristically imaginative style that, released by a well-known publisher, had sold through two printings nationally. A passage in the book recounted how Carlos had first heard from his father the story of the Irish girl and her mysterious French friend, the writer Chateaubriand.[2]

According to the intergenerational oral history, the story begins with a girl, as good stories must. Mary O'Neill, about twelve years old, lived in London sometime in the 1790s, Carlos said his father had told him. Although this was a time before picnics were acceptable for polite society, she would often leave school at midday and take her lunch to a nearby park. One day in the park she saw a gentleman, or so she assumed from his bearing, although he was obviously down on his luck. His clothes were tattered, his eyes sunken, his cheeks gaunt, and his hands trembling. So she offered him some of her meal. At first he politely refused, but eventually he succumbed, and accepted the food. Mary recognized right away that he was French. Indeed, in those days of revolutionary tumult in France, there were many destitute French aristocrats in London.

The next day she returned bearing lunch for two, and they met again. After several days, she asked her family if she might offer the spare room in the attic to the poor gentleman, who obviously needed a place to stay. Initially, Mary's request was met with resistance, since the attic room was to be kept available for newcomers from Ireland who needed temporary lodging while looking for work. But since the space was currently empty Mary ultimately prevailed. With permission granted, the stranger moved in and proved an exemplary boarder. He stayed for several months, supporting himself through writing and translating essays for French papers in London, then he moved on.

Some years later Mary blossomed into the loveliest young woman in the city, as girls often do in family tales. An Irishman named Patrick Fallon courted her, swept her off her feet, and married her. Shortly thereafter a son was born, whom they named Thomas. The Frenchman unexpectedly reappeared about this time, around 1800. He had determined that the terror in France was subsiding and he could now return with reasonable prospects of safety, so he wanted to say good-bye to the young girl who had saved him. Struck by the beauty of the woman she had become, he congratulated her on her marriage and her lively baby. Then, moved by the encounter, he exclaimed, "To thank you for rescuing me in my hour of need, let me undertake the responsibility of providing an education for your firstborn son!" He then returned to France.

When Mary and Patrick's son, Thomas, finished primary school, the Frenchman, François-René de Chateaubriand, was duly notified. Thomas Fallon was then sent to the Collège Royal of Amiens, France, where he received a first-class education provided through the largesse of Chateaubriand, who had been granted the title of viscount in 1815 by King Louis XVIII. The Frenchman's affection for the boy did not end with support of his education. In 1822, after Thomas had finished college at Amiens and returned to London, Chateaubriand arrived there as French ambassador. During the summer, he apparently commissioned an oil portrait of the young man, which he presented to him. When Chateaubriand left in the fall, according to my father, he made a gift to Thomas of his horse. Later Thomas, while riding the horse in Ireland, was stopped by the British police and asked to show that he had paid a tax on the horse. "No," Thomas replied, "I don't pay taxes to the English king, and neither does my horse, who is named 'Georgie' after the present king, George Three-and-a-Half, who presumes to call himself George IV yet has shown that he is but half a king." Thomas seems to have lost the horse in that exchange.

The family's oral history continued with exploits of Thomas and his descendants, right down to my father's life events. Missing from the story, however, was clarity about the nature of Chateaubriand's relationship to Mary O'Neill and Thomas, although tender reminiscences of Mary lingered over generations in our family, as well as admiration for the Frenchman and his support of Thomas's education, reflected in part by the fact that my grandfather retained in his library all of Chateaubriand's published works.

I knew from my father's storytelling that Thomas had emigrated from England to Colombia around 1830 and had married a beautiful, compassionate creole woman there, Doña Marcela Carrión de León y Armero. At first, Thomas had supervised the silver and gold mines in Tolima province, eventually becoming mining engineer for all the mines in the Republic of Colombia, including the emerald mines in Muzo, the coal mines in Nemocón, and the salt mines in Zipaquirá, serving successively each president of the developing nation. Thomas and Marcela had had three children. Two daughters, born in 1832 and 1836, had died of typhoid fever in their twenties. Thomas and Marcela had died within a few months of each other in 1863, leaving their son, Diego, born in 1834, bereft of his childhood family in the New World on the eve of his thirtieth birthday.

Diego Fallon became a nationally revered poet of Colombia, one of the forerunners of the style known as magical realism in modern Latin American literature. His son Diego José, called Dieguito—my grandfather—had pursued a career as a diplomat in the service of his country. My father, Carlos, had been head of the Colombian Navy at the time of my birth in Cartagena, before we left for North America, which is how I came to be raised in an aspiring middle-class immigrant family in the United States.

Now, in the remains of carefully guarded, timeworn letters, my father had provided me with a material gift concerning our ancestry, mediated through five generations. It was as if my dying father had passed me a baton for the next leg of a genealogical marathon whose goal was to clarify the past to enlighten the present. What was I to make of this apparent challenge?

At first, I felt a surge of responsibility. My father's weak handwriting seemed almost a plea: *Don't let these documents disappear!* Then I recognized the familiar pull of curiosity: Why had these letters survived so many generations? What had led Chateaubriand to write to my great-great-grandfather Thomas Fallon? How had Chateaubriand directly or indirectly affected the arc of the family from which I had descended? Could I trust the stories my father had so vividly related? Finally, having dedicated my life to serving my colleagues in the academy, I heard the call of scholarly duty. These letters were important artifacts that would surely shed light on the biography of a famous historical figure. Ultimately, these fragments of letters from a time long gone called me to make sense of the story of Viscount Chateaubriand and the Irish girl.

To begin, I needed to quench a curiosity about François-René de Chateaubriand. To most speakers of English, his family name suggests, if anything, a steak recipe. It is true that Chateaubriand was a notable epicure, having secured the lifelong personal services of a chef widely regarded as the best in Europe. More importantly, he was also an ambitious adventurer, a flamboyant diplomat, and a gifted writer regarded as the founder of modern French literature. He left an indelible mark not only on the society of his time and on admirers who have discovered him since, but on five generations of the family into which I was born.

The colorful recitations of the Chateaubriand story within my family were surely based on something that really happened, I thought. Nonetheless, I knew that an honest account begun by forebears could be unwittingly and cumulatively reshaped through retelling over generations as details lost through layered forgetting were perhaps embellished with patches of imagination wrought to hold the story together. Driven to learn more as accurately as I could, I began my quest by engaging the charismatic Frenchman directly.

CHAPTER 2

Discovering Chateaubriand

ADVENTURE AWAITS.

To pursue my quest for answers to the mysteries posed by my family story and the centuries-old letters given to me by my father, I needed to explore the times, places, and sensibilities that shaped Chateaubriand's approach to his world, as well as the works he wrote about his life experiences. Pouring myself into the forty-two volumes of Chateaubriand's most influential work, *Mémoires d'outre-tombe*, seemed a good launching ramp for my search. The confidently self-aware writer penned the title of this literary autobiography, usually translated as *Memoirs from Beyond the Grave*, after making certain that his life's lyrical recollections would be published only after his death. Needing more perspective, I followed up by reading other works by the master wordsmith and many works about him and the time in which he lived. I also corresponded with noted Chateaubriand scholars and mined documents in archives and libraries, wherever I could find them.

Like most scholars who investigate the past, I was reminded that history is imperfectly disciplined by evidence. The reconstruction of a life from long ago is inevitably at least partly an act of imagination. Hard facts, often revealed in documents of the time, are essential, and every instance must be considered. Nonetheless, riddles stubbornly tease us. The evidence we discover is never enough to satisfy all we would like to know. Beyond the uneven nature of the facts themselves lie the many voids for which we have no clues. To arrange what we know in a persuasively plausible pattern, we must interpret all that we have found. A major challenge is seeking to recapture the ways people of another time and place experienced the world around them. To pursue my quest for answers to the mystery posed by my family story, anchored by signed letters from 1817, I sought to explore the times, places, and sensibilities that shaped Chateaubriand's approach to his world. I needed to know him as best I could.

A summary of what I understand about Chateaubriand's life and times provides the backdrop for the story told about Chateaubriand and the Irish girl by my ancestors with both intrigue and endearment, embodying themes that also recur throughout generations of my family's history. It's a concise account of a fascinating person who lived life for the purpose of telling it, and who happened to be alive during perhaps the most formative decades in the recent history of Western civilization.

Now, more than three hundred years since the reign of Louis XIV, fabulous Sun King, builder of Versailles, and benefactor of Molière, Racine, Lully, LeBrun, and Couperin, memories of his court still endure as a symbol of the glory of France. Convinced of the divine right of kings, Louis XIV stood on a political summit whose precarious steepness was hidden from practically all observers. Aristocratic European society embraced King Louis XIV's vision of the monarchical organization of society. Yet little more than half a century after his death in 1715, ominous signs of an impending shift from the established order were increasingly apparent, though ignored by those intent on preserving the status quo.

The leakage of power from the throne could have been detected by observing the gains of scheming ambitious rulers of minor fiefdoms or by considering the consciousness developing among the common people, implicit citizens of an emergent modern state. Unwillingness of the masses to remain abject subjects of a supreme monarch portended severe consequences for society and was a thought best avoided by those who had accustomed themselves to life as they found it. Therefore, even long after the Sun King's departure few sensed that the era of powerful monarchy was in its twilight. Confusion and uncertainty seemed to lurk along the boundaries between human beings fated to their station in society and those seeking the alluring promise of universal autonomy.

In a world where such fragile social unease hid beneath the surface of a long taken-for-granted hierarchical order, Apolline de Bëdée, the forty-two-year-old wife of René-Auguste de Chateaubriand, was seized by the labor that began the birth of her eleventh and last child. An ominous storm lashed at the ramparts of the usually charming Breton seaport of Saint-Malo as Madame Chateaubriand moved with her fifty-year-old husband and household into new quarters adjacent to the wall surrounding the old city. She then promptly retired to an upstairs back room in full view of the now churning, seemingly endless sea to complete her arduous appointment with childbirth. Meteorologists confirm that the epic rain, which lasted for nearly a month, appeared to reach its height on the morning of September 4, 1768, when the infant François-René, upon entering the world, made his first audible cry.

Although four children had died in infancy, and another was miscarried, six survived to adulthood, including François-René, who had a brother, Jean-Baptiste, nine years older, and four sisters, Marie Anne, Bénigne, Julie, and Lucile, who were eight, seven, five, and four years older. The infant François-René was quickly dispatched to a wet nurse in the village where an uncle lived, many miles away, thus initiating a sense of exile that would accompany him throughout his long life. Exile seemed agreeable to him; as an adult he would reminisce about his early childhood years spent happily in the countryside of Brittany. Three years later François-René was returned to his mother. Now a toddler, he played with other children in the streets of Saint-Malo; as he grew, he came to love the drama of the extreme tides convulsed by the sea of that region during long walks on the beach; exulted with the shorebirds full of life and flying free; accepted as a fact of life the looming cathedral that dominated the town with its smells, sounds, and sacraments; and came to terms with a household comprised of daunting, if somewhat distant, parents and older sisters who provided much of his parenting.

François-René's father, René-Auguste, was a taciturn man driven by a singular ambition. He carried the distinguished name Chateaubriand, descended from ancestors who had fought with William the Conqueror at the Battle of Hastings and had accompanied King Louis IX, later canonized as Saint Louis, on two crusades. Over generations, however, the estates supporting the nobility of the house of Chateaubriand had been lost through profligacy, foolish choices, the vagaries of fate, and absorption by marriage into another family, the House of Condé. Having been born into a household with few resources, whose meager inheritance he had to share with three brothers, René-Auguste was sharply focused on regaining what he considered his rightful status as a nobleman by acquiring a landed estate. As a means to this end, he turned to the sea.

With neither wealth nor aristocratic connections to secure a commission in the Royal Navy, René-Auguste went to sea at age fifteen as a common sailor from the port of Saint-Malo. Being frugal, disciplined, and a steady learner, by age twenty-eight he became a captain; soon after, he was able to purchase his first ship and, in time, others. After several voyages under his command, he settled in Saint-Malo and managed his ships and merchant trade from his office.

From his seafaring business ventures, René-Auguste became prosperous and succeeded by age forty-four in acquiring for a large sum the dark castle of Combourg. Located in central Brittany, it included feudal estates and serfs, whose labor in the fields provided an annual income. Henceforth, by law and tradition, he could add several titles to his name, including Count of Combourg. At the time of François-René's birth, René-Auguste had already begun spending considerable time at Combourg, returning to Saint-Malo for as long as half a year but gradually less and less.

François-René began his elementary education in Saint-Malo, where he attended a day school run by a priest associated with the local Benedictine monastery. When François-René was nine years old, his father decided to retire to Combourg and live out his years there as a country gentleman managing his estate. So on May 14, 1777, in a gilded carriage drawn by eight horses, François-René set off with his mother and sisters to join his father in Combourg. He was soon enrolled at a well-regarded boarding school in the nearby town of Dol, where he excelled, especially in mathematics, then at age twelve began attending secondary school in Rennes, where he also was at the top of his class. Less than two years later, at age fourteen, he was sent to Brest, on the west coast of Brittany, in hopes of receiving a commission to join the Royal Navy.

Life as a cadet-in-waiting was a less than satisfying pastime since becoming a cadet depended on the needs of the navy. One afternoon in June 1783 François-René witnessed a fleet of ships entering the harbor with all sails aloft, flags and banners waving, and cannons booming in celebration of the end of the long war with England. France, having lost much of its territory in North America to England in the Seven Years' War, now—after helping the new colonists in North America break free from England to establish their own independent republic—had achieved some measure of satisfaction. The costs of war, however, had begun to raise the specter of national bankruptcy, thus exacerbating the conditions that would soon engulf French society in a shattering revolution. François-René drew his own conclusion: with war at an end, the likelihood of a commission in the Royal Navy was small to nonexistent. He quietly gathered his belongings; notified no one, not even his parents; and headed home to Combourg.

His parents understood the disappointing realities he faced on the eve of his fifteenth birthday and welcomed him back to the castle. Unsure of what he was to become, and perhaps to please his mother, François-René abruptly announced his wish to pursue a career in the Church. His parents found this a happy solution and arranged his enrollment in the seminary in the town of Dinan. There he spent a term perfecting his command of Latin and Greek and learning a bit of Hebrew, but mostly playing hooky, spending long periods of time at the estate of an uncle nearby or visiting Combourg.

François-René's experience in Dinan made clear that theology was not his calling, thus bringing his formal education to a close in spring 1784. He returned to Combourg to spend his time in self-study, bucolic pursuits, and anticipation of manhood. His brother, Jean-Baptiste, was in Paris, well on his way to a successful career in law, and his three eldest sisters had married, leaving

François-René to live out his adolescence in the castle with his remaining sister Lucile and his aging remote parents.

Within his family circle, François-René permitted himself an occasional sense of resentment. As the youngest, it seemed to him that attention, affection, and understanding were directed more toward his older siblings, especially Jean Baptiste, who by birth order as well as gender was principal heir. From his parents, François-René detected little expectation in the way of plans or training for where his own life might lead. He was left to imagine his own ambition. François-René was by all reports a superior student and an inquisitive learner, absorbing deeply the lessons and culture of the day, but he was not bookish and aloof. He had childhood friends, some of whom remained close well onto his early adulthood. His play was often rambunctious and even dangerous. In allegiance to his friends, he engaged enthusiastically in fights with groups perceived as hostile, and responded aggressively when attacked. Always, even at such times, he was a keen observer, leading him to a sense of separateness from the world while living squarely in the midst of it.

So it was that François-René came of age in the gloomy fortress of Combourg. His close companion, Lucile, would turn twenty that first summer, one month before his sixteenth birthday. His parents followed a strict routine. In the winter months, after the sun had set early, supper was served at 8:00 p.m. Afterward, the four family members would sit quietly in the parlor, dimly lit by firelight. François-René and Lucile would whisper quietly to each other, while their mother would sigh in her chair, pursuing her embroidery or some other solitary pastime. Their father would roam endlessly around the room. Years later, François-René recalled these evenings in his memoirs.

It was then that my father began a stroll that did not cease until he went to bed. He was dressed in a thick white woolen gown, or rather a sort of cloak, such as I have never seen on anybody but him, and he covered his half-bald head with a tall white cap that stood straight up. When, in the course of this stroll, he moved away from the hearth, the hall was so dimly lit, by a single candle, that he was no longer visible. Only his footsteps could still be heard in the darkness. Then, slowly, he would return toward the light, emerging little by little from the shadows, like a specter, with his white gown, his white cap, and his long pale face. Lucile and I exchanged a few whispered words while he was at the far end of the hall, but we fell silent as soon as he came near. He asked, as he passed us: "What are you two chattering about?" Terror stricken, we made no reply. My father continued on his walk. For the rest of the evening, nothing could be heard but the measured sound of his footsteps, my mother's sighs, and the murmuring of the wind.[1]

Aside from occasional adventures with the gamekeeper on the estate, François-René's life at Combourg became largely internalized, enlivened by his adolescent imagination. It was here that he was first visited by his Sylphide, an imaginary idealized feminine spirit who invariably appeared when he was seized by intense sexual energy but also at other times, for comfort or reassurance. His sexual awakening was no doubt enhanced by the close companionship of Lucile, with her supportive responses to his observations about the world around him and her own struggle with a journey toward unknowable adulthood. We may never learn the extent of the intimacy between these siblings, although some scholars and critics have speculated incest, a theme not uncommon in late-eighteenth-century European literature—for example, the popular 1788 novel *Paul et Virgenie* by Jacques-Henri Bernardin de Saint-Pierre, about a couple, unrelated by blood but close friends from birth, raised by two widows as if they were brother and sister, who eventually fall in love. Since they are unrelated, their feelings for each other are not actually incestuous, though inevitably their mothers act as if their mutual attraction is dangerous, with, in the end, tragic consequences. In a complementary way, although it is unlikely that Chateaubriand and Lucile committed incest, they may have felt in their shared adolescent world closer than an ordinary sister and brother, and perhaps sensed a cloud of worry about the prospect of mortal sin.

Indiscreet interest in the relationship between Lucile and François-René may not have arisen were it not for his immensely popular second novella, *René,* initially published in 1802. In it, a disillusioned Frenchman, René, seeking solace among North American Indians, is coaxed into telling his life story, which centers on his sister Amélie, who suffers from unbearable guilt over some sin—a character who, by Chateaubriand's own admission, was modeled on Lucile. Amélie retreats to a convent, and during the ceremony to confirm her vows, René, as the family member responsible for giving her to the Church, describes this climactic moment:

> I was constrained to kneel beside this lugubrious scene. Suddenly a confusing mumble arose from beneath the sepulchral veil; I leaned forward and these dreadful words (which I alone heard) struck my ear: "God of pity, grant that I may never rise from this funereal bed, and bestow Thy blessings on a brother who did not share my criminal passion!"[2]

This is hardly a confession of incest, although in the context of a story replete with declarations of love and affection on both sides, and with so many autobiographical allusions, it was bound to raise eyebrows. There is, in fact, no convincing evidence of carnal love between Chateaubriand and his sister.

Lucile was, however, an important influence on Chateaubriand during his adolescence. He luxuriated in long walks over the estate with her, marveling at the beauty of the natural world; at such times, his descriptions about what he experienced and how he felt were so richly poetic that she told him he should write them down. Subsequently, they both began writing poems and essays they then shared with each other, so much so that Chateaubriand credits Lucile with setting him on the path to his career as a writer. In his memoirs, he wrote, "It was in the woods of Combourg that I became what I am."[3]

Chateaubriand's idylls in Combourg ended abruptly in summer 1786, when, at age seventeen, he was summoned to his father's room one morning at 8:00. René-Auguste, sensing that he had not much longer to live, had reasoned that the boy needed a suitable career right away and, without informing him, had written to François-René's brother, Jean-Baptiste, now a lawyer with many connections in Paris, to seek a position for the boy as an officer in the Royal Army. Accordingly, François-René was to proceed to Paris and from there to Cambrai to join the regiment of Navarre. François-René was ushered at that very moment to a waiting carriage, leaving Combourg and his youth behind. In September 1786, just before his eighteenth birthday, upon his induction into the regiment, he received news that his father had suffered a stroke and died. In accordance with custom and law, the estate at Combourg was left to the eldest son, Jean-Baptiste. René-Auguste's widow received an annual pension, but François-René and his sisters inherited virtually nothing.

Chateaubriand advanced rapidly through the ranks in his regiment, from enlistee to corporal, to sergeant, then to second lieutenant.

Jean-Baptiste, wanting to ensure success for his younger brother, arranged for him to be inducted into the Knights of Malta and presented at the court of King Louis XVI as the Chevalier de Chateaubriand. Although he acquiesced in his brother's efforts to ensure his status as a representative of the nobility, Chateaubriand found the social requirements uncomfortable. He preferred to retreat into his own melancholy, finding comfort in isolating himself from the world. Because no wars were imminent and the state treasury was bare, the army was more than happy to grant its soldiers ample periods of leave, thus permitting Chateaubriand time to experience Paris, introduce himself to established writers he admired, and observe the city's increasingly dramatic, often violent, and decidedly unpredictable politics.

Chateaubriand found himself in the midst of events that triggered the French Revolution. Indeed, many historians agree that actions of the parliament in Brittany in 1788 helped set in motion the inexorable fall of royalist France. The king's government needed to raise taxes to save the nation, but such measures were unpopular. The parliament in Brittany was among the first to spurn the government's edicts. Dominated by the nobility, the parliament rejected, among other indignities, a proposal to end the exemption of nobles from taxes. Nineteen-year-old Chateaubriand, nobleman from Combourg, participated in the assembly and supported its actions. Although his sympathies lay more with reformers than reactionaries, he was delighted to be engaged with affairs of state. Decades later, as a mature writer, he would calmly reflect, "Patricians started the revolution and plebeians finished it."[4]

The events begun in Brittany resulted ultimately in the king's dismissal of the government, the installation of politicians more palatable to the nobility, and the summoning of the Estates General, last invoked in 1614, to consider reforms and solutions. This medieval assemblage consisted of three groups: nobility, clergy, and the commons, representatives of the people who were neither noble nor clerical. Nobility and clergy made up a two-thirds majority and thus customarily determined outcomes, but this time the commons, angered by poverty and powerlessness, chose not to play by the rules, declaring themselves the only legitimate representatives of citizens of France, commandeering the Estates General, pushing aside the nobility and the clergy, and ushering in the revolution. Chateaubriand was in Paris on July 14, 1789, where, following the crowd, he observed the disorderly "liberation" of the Bastille.

Along with so many of his countrymen, Chateaubriand did not know quite what to make of the revolution. He later wrote, "In a society that is dissolving and recomposing itself... the human race on holiday strolls down the street, rid of its masters, restored for a moment to its natural state."[5] Although castigated by his brother for being a moderate because he saw value in some reforms sought by the revolutionaries, Chateaubriand was revolted by the violence, especially the seemingly unending specter of heads on pikes. As he put it, "These heads, and others that I would encounter soon after, changed my political leanings; I was horrified by these cannibal feasts, and the idea of leaving France for some distant country began to take root in my mind."[6] Unable to resolve the conflict about where to place his allegiance, he deftly chose to get away.

Chateaubriand was fascinated by the mystery of the New World on the other side of the Atlantic. At one time, he had happily entertained his brother's plan to send him to the French outpost of Saint-Domingue, today's Haiti, to collect old debts owed to their father, but the idea came to nothing. Now his reading and conversations with elder Frenchmen he met in Paris led him to imagine that he could serve the glory of France and satisfy his own sense of adventure by seeking the rumored Northwest Passage, from the newly formed United States of America to the Pacific Ocean. He secured funds from his brother, made appropriate arrangements, and on the evening of April 7, 1791, at age twenty-two, set sail on the *Saint-Pierre* from the port of Saint-Malo.

The eternal, ever-undulating sea was his longtime friend, rewarding him by shielding him from seasickness, even when almost all other passengers succumbed. Not only did the sea connect the European Old World with the American New World but it impressed him as enduring all that had come before and all that might ever be. Clutching his small copy of Homer's *Odyssey*, he reveled in the storms. Years later, one of the passengers, an abbé named Édouard de Mondésir, reported that during one violent storm Chateaubriand, imitating Odysseus, had himself lashed tightly to the forward mast of the vessel as it was being thrown about violently by cascading waters on the open ocean amid pouring rain, thunder, and lightning, shouting, "O Tempest, thou art still not so glorious as Homer portrays thee!"[7] Since the image of being lashed to a mast during a storm at sea was common in the romantic era, especially in paintings, we cannot be sure this incident actually occurred, but one thing is certain: Chateaubriand was thrilled being at sea and on his own in the world.

Chateaubriand's sojourn in North America was brief but rewarding in exotic experiences that filled the reservoir of his imagination, inspiring narratives and novellas destined to make him famous. He disembarked in Baltimore on Sunday, July 10, 1791, and made his way toward Philadelphia, where he hoped to meet George Washington, to whom he was carrying a letter of introduction; but Washington, ill at that time, was unable to receive visitors. From Philadelphia, Chateaubriand traveled to New York; made a brief round trip to Boston, cradle of the American Revolution; and then continued by sloop up the Hudson

River to Albany, considered a gateway to the West. He hired a guide of Dutch descent who spoke several Indian languages; bought provisions and two horses; and set out along the Iroquois Trail toward Niagara Falls. There he was so captivated by the majesty of the cascade that he attempted to descend to its base on a worn ladder of vines fashioned by local Indians but fell to a ledge, breaking his left arm. His guide brought a band of Indians who then lifted Chateaubriand with a birch-bark rope and took him to a nearby Huron encampment, where the natives set his arm and kept him for almost two weeks, entertaining him from time to time with song and dance. His American adventure was well launched.

Over the next several weeks, Chateaubriand traveled by river and over portages southward toward Fort Pitt, today's city of Pittsburgh. He then crossed the western boundary of the recently formed United States of America and proceeded down the Ohio River toward its mouth, where it converges with the great Mississippi River. Along the way, he realized the impracticality of searching for a route to the Pacific Ocean and, seeing that the funds for his trip were depleting more rapidly than planned, determined that he would have to return to France before the winter snows. In the meantime, he made the most of his journey, befriending peddlers, traders, colorful Seminole Indians who had come north from Florida, and fellow countrymen on their way to the outpost of St. Louis.

After seeing the Mississippi River, near today's Cairo, Illinois, he turned back up the Ohio River, along the Tennessee and Cumberland Rivers to Nashville, over the wilderness trail to Knoxville, and via what was called the Great Valley Road, or the Great Trading Path, through Virginia and on to the Northeast. Near Abingdon, while taking refuge for a night at a farmer's homestead, he saw by firelight a broadside that passed for a newspaper, with the headline: "Flight of the King." The lead story reported that Louis XVI and Marie Antoinette had sought to flee France but had been discovered, arrested, and returned to Paris. This news fortified Chateaubriand's conviction to return soon to France to do what he could to save his homeland. After possibly meeting President Washington, he set sail for France from Philadelphia on December 10, 1791.

Upon setting foot on French soil at Le Havre on January 2, 1792, Chateaubriand headed for Saint-Malo, where his mother and Lucile had returned after leaving Combourg upon the death of René-Auguste. In Chateaubriand's absence, they had determined that since he had hardly any money, his only hope for the future lay in marriage to someone of wealth; and they had found the perfect choice, Lucile's friend Céleste Buisson de la Vigne, an eighteen-year-old of high standing who was rumored to be on the verge of inheriting a fortune from an aging grandfather.

True to his frequent pattern of succumbing to what life presented, Chateaubriand committed what he later described as "the gravest act of my life." He married Céleste, confessing years later that "in order to avoid the quarrel of an hour, I would sell myself into slavery for a century."[8] Chateaubriand formally honored his marriage vow to Céleste throughout their long lives, although in their mature years they lived separately without physical intimacy, even in the same household. He respected Céleste and was grateful for her kindness, but she held no interest for him as a life partner or as a lover. For love, he turned to other women, serially engaging in multiple affairs. As it turned out, Céleste received no fortune after all, even though promised wealth would hardly have mattered at the height of the revolution. After a brief honeymoon in Brittany, the newlyweds moved to Paris, where Chateaubriand was soon to leave his bride for much longer than either of them had reason to imagine.

As the revolution began drifting toward its darkest days, faces of people on the streets of Paris were grim, angry, or fearful. To be sure, there was also enthusiasm, even joy, at the prospect of a new citizens' republic, but these sentiments seemed less spontaneous than obligatory. The sturdy guillotine, a marvel of new technology, was beginning to assume its commanding role. The foreboding atmosphere reinforced what Chateaubriand had already determined while sailing homeward from America—that his responsibility was to leave the crumbling mess that France had become and take up arms to invade it. Thus would the lawless crowds be subdued and the nation's soul be restored.

Nobility from Prussia, Austria, and the lowlands were assembling an "army of princes" to reestablish order in France. On the home front, the revolutionaries had begun disdainfully applying the label "émigré" to those who were, for whatever reason, abandoning France, considering them traitors and placing their names on "émigré lists" so they could be called to account should they return. Such danger did not concern François-René. Even if it had to come with help from an invading army, he was certain that order would soon be restored, clearing the aberrant rolling mist of cruelty seeping across his homeland.

His brother, Jean-Baptiste, had deeper roots in what would soon be called the *ancien régime*. Having inherited his father's obsession with their heritage of nobility, he had sought to consolidate the gains his father had made. He had studied law to bring himself into the circle of powerful advisers to the government. He had married well, into a family with broad diplomatic connections, insinuating himself into Parisian society, as well as among the courtiers surrounding the royal family. He was a monarchist, with everything to lose if the revolutionaries were to succeed and much to gain if the monarchy prevailed.

Though the brothers may have had different motivations for wanting to restore order and return the monarchy to France, they abruptly departed France together, leaving their wives behind, and for Jean-Baptiste also an infant son. Aiming to join the invading forces, they disappeared into the night disguised as wine merchants, headed for the border town of Lille carrying false passports that Jean-Baptiste had obtained. The following evening they walked across farm fields until they reached Belgium, where they introduced themselves to troops from the gathering army and then continued on to Brussels, where they parted. Jean-Baptiste's aristocratic connections secured him a position as aide-de-camp to his wife's great uncle, who commanded two light horse companies on what was planned as the northwestern wing of the invasion. François-René, happy to be a common soldier, took leave for the Rhine, where the larger army, under command of the king of Prussia, was assembling.

The bright visions of Chateaubriand and his compatriots were soon revealed as illusory. Chateaubriand's first inkling of impending doom came with the distribution of weapons, which turned out to be outmoded castoffs from the regular Prussian army. His own musket had a frozen hammer and was incapable of firing. The gentlemen officers who headed the brigades lodged their certainty of victory in tactics of bluff and bluster. Confident that the citizen defenders would run at the sight of massed troops carrying colorful battle flags under the command of elegantly uniformed generals on fine horses, they made few plans for actual battles, much less contingencies for setbacks.

The campaign began in mid-August and was over by October. The late summer and early autumn months were unusually wet, requiring much of the conflict to be fought in relentless rain. Chateaubriand's unit was assigned to take the border city of Thionville, or at least to besiege it so that its forces could not hinder the march on Paris farther to the northwest. All along the front, commanders were confused by what they encountered. Confounding aristocratic logic, the upstart citizens of the revolution were determined to defend their homeland. What was ordered as a swift attack and conquest turned instead into a brief siege followed quickly by humiliating defeat. The fighting at Thionville was intense, with opposing sides able to see and taunt each other while inflicting pain and death.

Wounded in the thigh by a shard from a shell exploding nearby, Chateaubriand was forced to retreat in disorderly flight with his compatriots. His wound became infected, impairing his ability to walk, and, due to a compromised immune system, he also acquired an illness characterized by fever and scarring, probably chicken pox. Nonetheless, despite his desperate condition, he managed to survive. Remembering that his mother's brother, Uncle Bédée, had told him he planned to escape the revolution by going to family property on the Channel Island of Jersey, Chateaubriand headed by canal barge to Oostende, then ferried to Jersey. The grand army of princes simply dissolved. Jean-Baptiste, still obdurately focused on protecting his hard-won nobility, managed to return safely to the castle in Combourg, bringing his wife and child with him. There he planned to defend his recently inherited estate holdings.

Uncle Bédée welcomed François-René into his family on Jersey, where the young adventurer, initially hovering between life and death, slowly recuperated over several months. Bédée arrived one day in late January 1793 dressed in mourning clothes to inform him that the king had met his fate on the guillotine. The elegant elderly aristocrat Malesherbes, whose granddaughter was Jean-Baptiste's wife, had passionately defended the king before the revolutionary tribunal, even though Malesherbes was well known as a critic of royal abuse and a leading figure of enlightenment thought. Nonetheless, by serving his king, Malesherbes was now himself likely a target for execution, Chateaubriand realized, along with his immediate relatives, including perhaps Jean-Baptiste.

As the revolution progressed in France, what little wealth remained for Bëdée and the surviving members of the Chateaubriand family was gradually confiscated, making clear to François-René the burden his continued presence imposed on the Bëdée household. Returning to France, possibly to fight with ragtag counterrevolutionary militias, was no reasonable option. Instead, temporary exile to England, where a credible army of émigrés might eventually be assembled, seemed to him the only alternative. Therefore, in mid-May Chateaubriand left Jersey, sailing north and east toward Southampton, the gateway port to London.

Although the voyage was short, once again the brooding sea comforted him. On board, Chateaubriand befriended a fellow nobleman he had met at the parliament in Rennes, François-Marie Hingant de la Tiemblais. Since neither had much in the way of cash reserves, they were forced to travel from Southampton to London by common wagons shared with sailors, a journey of three days. Upon disembarking, Chateaubriand was spitting blood and feverish. A physician gave him little chance of survival beyond a few months. Even if it seemed as though his very being was at risk, his personality was now fully formed and scraps of nascent manuscripts were tucked into his meager belongings, auguring that his exile in England could confidently set him on a path to the future he had long imagined would bring him renown.

The substantial community of French émigrés in London proved helpful to Chateaubriand in finding a room to rent at only six shillings a month. His friend from the crossing, Hingant, had a room not far away, allowing the two of them to share breakfast regularly, conversing mostly about the calamity their homeland had become. In a matter of weeks, Chateaubriand also befriended the charismatic Jean Gabriel Peltier, who had achieved success in London as a journalist catering to the émigré community with newsletters and books. He was immediately attracted to Chateaubriand's literary intelligence, and Chateaubriand saw in Peltier an opportunity to get his ideas in print. The inspiration that had recently seized Chateaubriand's imagination was to write a definitive history of revolutions from ancient times to the present, a project he believed might bring opposing sides in France to see possibilities for reconciliation. Peltier enthusiastically endorsed the project; moved Chateaubriand to a modest room at Cox, Son and Baylis, the establishment that published his newsletters; and occasionally provided him with cash in exchange for translation and other work as he focused on his writing.

While he wrote translations by day and his essay on revolutions at night, Chateaubriand's health continued to deteriorate, eventually limiting his ability to work and reducing his small sporadic income, thus compounding his illness with the specter of hunger. For five days, both he and Hingant went without food, surviving on water and herbs, or grass, from lawns and gardens. Hingant, who sometimes seemed giddy to the point of instability, then attempted suicide.

Chateaubriand discovered Hingant's stab wound and saved his life by getting him to physicians in the émigré community. At this desperate moment toward the end of summer, Chateaubriand received 120 francs from his still struggling family in Brittany, sent via his Uncle Bëdée on Jersey. With this small monetary infusion, Chateaubriand was able to pay his back rent and other outstanding debts, and move, in fall 1793, to a less expensive but adequate attic garret in the St. Marylebone Parish of London. There he regained his health, continued writing his essay, and began to develop the prose works that had fired his imagination before and during his trip to America, which would eventually become part of a collection, *Les Natchez*, containing the novellas *Atala* and *René*.

Late in 1793 Chateaubriand moved from London to Beccles, in Suffolk, where he assumed the post of French teacher at the local school, a position he regarded as demeaning. He had hoped to be employed as translator of old French Norman documents for a town history project, but that proved illusory. At least the school provided a salary sufficient for his upkeep. Because his name was difficult for the English to pronounce, he introduced himself to his students and others as M. de Combourg. Nonetheless, the boys in his class learned his actual family name, pronouncing it in their own jocular way as "Shatterbrain," further increasing his sense of isolation and disempowerment.

After living in Beccles less than five months, he was having dinner alone at a tavern where a patron was reading to his companions from a newspaper reporting on the latest horrors in France. The names of individuals decapitated by guillotine in recent days were listed—among them, M. Malesherbes, who had defended the king, and also his daughter and grandchildren, the Count and Countess de Chateaubriand. Learning in this chance way about the gruesome death of his brother, Chateaubriand rose from the table, nearly fainted, and stumbled out to the street.

The next year, the school in Beccles closed. It was 1795, and Chateaubriand, relieved of his teaching position there, was by now well connected as a tutor of French language and literature. After being slightly injured from a fall off his horse, he was taken in by John Ives, the parson in the village of Bungay, six miles from Beccles, and given lodging and meals in return for intellectual conversation with Parson Ives and French lessons for the parson's daughter, Charlotte, who was about to turn sixteen.

In his memoirs, Chateaubriand describes a deep love affair with young Charlotte Ives. It was dashed with searing quickness after less than a year, when Mrs. Ives told him late one evening that she and the parson had noticed the growing affection between the couple and would be pleased to welcome him into their family. Chateaubriand recounted the consequence of this unexpected turn of events:

> Of all the painful things that I had endured, this was the greatest and most wounding. I threw myself on my knees at Mrs. Ives' feet and covered her hands with kisses and tears. She thought I was weeping with happiness and started sobbing with joy.…"Stop!" I cried. "I am married!" Mrs. Ives fell back in a faint.[9]

With that exclamation, he rushed from the house, alternately ran and limped the six miles to Beccles, and took the next carriage coach to London, arriving there in late 1796.

As Chateaubriand settled once again in the big city, he continued writing and expanded his circle of acquaintances within the community of French exiles. The essay on revolutions, written in segments over several years beginning in 1793, was published in 1797, first in London and later in Paris. It was a curious work for a royalist, expressing seeming approval of revolutionary ideas, criticism of the Catholic Church, and skepticism about the divinity of Christ. Propelled by its audacious and brilliant style, the essay won wide popularity and earned Chateaubriand a measure of renown.

In 1798, Chateaubriand learned in a letter from his sister Julie that his mother had died. Although it is unlikely that either his mother or his sisters had read the essay on revolutions, they had surely heard about it, since it was widely discussed in France at the time. In the letter, Julie upbraided her brother, writing that his mother had been deeply offended by his seeming impiety, carrying her disappointment for the few remaining months of her life. Upon learning of his mother's lonely death, and feeling that he had inadvertently betrayed her, he experienced in a flash what he called a conversion experience and began a new essay, to which he gave the title "The Genius of Christianity."

Meanwhile, the execution of the revolutionary ideologue Robespierre and the mitigation of the Reign of Terror led to signs of normalization in France, even as the government remained disorderly and unpredictable. The army, under the brilliant young commander Napoleon, helped consolidate the gains of the revolution, and in November 1799 he succeeded in overthrowing the weak and despotic republican government. Order was thus restored, even if the outcome resembled a de facto dictatorship. Given the relative calm, in early May 1800 Chateaubriand decided to return to France, initially under an assumed name, with a forged passport identifying him as a Swiss citizen.

Once more in Paris, Chateaubriand sought to build upon the success he had achieved with his essay on revolutions. In addition to his ongoing work on Christianity, he had now completed two novellas. One, *Atala*, was set in America and described the doomed love between a half-caste Indian woman and an Indian man raised by a Spaniard. The other, *René*, which was semiautobiographical, focused on a young French Breton named René, who found ancient and modern Europe unwelcoming, summoning melancholy and irrelevance. The protagonist's one joy was companionship with his sister, who abandoned him to become a nun. Learning that she sought the convent to expiate guilt over her incestuous desire for him, René fled to America to live with Indians and, after learning of his sister's death, was killed in an Indian battle.

The way Chateaubriand animated characters in his stories revealed his personality. As with his character René, events and the world simply happened to Chateaubriand; ultimately, he would act decisively, but usually after perception and reflection—that is, in reaction, rather than in swashbuckling or impetuous advances. It was by commenting on events with personal insight and imaginatively skilled language that Chateaubriand constructed his art.

Because each of Chateaubriand's novellas contained Christian themes, he considered including them as chapters in his essay on Christianity. Nonetheless, since that work was not quite finished and he wanted to consolidate his reputation as a writer, he decided to release *Atala* right away, publishing it in April 1801. Pathbreaking in style and content, it was an immediate success like no other recent literary offering, reprinted five times in less than a year, adapted for both stage and opera, rendered into song on the streets of France, and regarded even today as a key stepping-stone to what would soon be called French romantic literature.

At this time Napoleon, as first consul, was embarking on a political initiative to reconcile the new French republic with the Catholic Church. Soon after, in April 1802, Chateaubriand published *The Genius of Christianity*, which included both *Atala* and *René*, artfully dedicating it to the first consul. The view of Christianity it presented had little to do with theology. Instead, here Chateaubriand extolled the importance of living by rules that speak to universal human values and help cement society. He also praised aspects of church rituals, writing of the joy of religion, with its majestic cathedrals and beautiful ceremonies incorporating splendid sights, sounds, and ancient incantations that move the spirit. The noted Chateaubriand scholar Irving Putter stressed that the work was a poet's argument about the artistry of Catholicism. Putter summarized it pithily, stating that for Chateaubriand, Christianity was "a religion of bells and incense."[10] Chateaubriand's emergence as a literary lion, and one of the republic's most prominent citizens, resulted in the first portrait of him as an adult, painted around 1808 by Anne-Louis Girodet de Roussy-Trioson (see figure 1).

Napoleon, who was but one year younger than Chateaubriand, wasted no time in conspicuously appointing him to a position of great importance in the government, initiating a diplomatic career that lasted more than a generation. Chateaubriand served the first consul as secretary to the ambassador to Rome, among other assignments, before resigning courageously and dramatically in 1804, when Napoleon, on fabricated charges, kidnapped the Duke of Enghien, a relative of the Bourbon heirs to the throne living in Germany, and had him executed.

With time on his hands, Chateaubriand traveled eastward through Greece, home of classic writers and philosophers, to the Holy Sepulchre in Jerusalem, an adventure that lasted more than a year. He then traveled homeward via North Africa and Spain, where he joined his current mistress, one of several with whom he partnered from Parisian society. Upon Napoleon's first defeat in 1814, Chateaubriand published a perfectly timed pamphlet, *Of Bonaparte and the Bourbons*, critical of Napoleon and anticipating the benefits inherent in the return of Bourbon royalty.

Principled opposition to Napoleon positioned Chateaubriand neatly for service to King Louis XVIII upon the first restoration of the monarchy in France, in 1814. At the second restoration, in 1815, following the decisive defeat of Napoleon at Waterloo, the king rewarded Chateaubriand by making him a lord, thus a member of parliament, and conferring upon him the royal title of viscount.

Chateaubriand proved to be a controversially flamboyant diplomat, alternately gaining and losing the king's favor. He was relieved of his duties and thus publicly humiliated by the king in September 1816 after publishing a pamphlet critical of royal policies. The resulting loss of income proved unexpectedly devastating. Chateaubriand was forced to sell first his personal library and then his beloved home in the Valley of the Wolves, outside Paris. Having no fixed abode, he visited the homes of friends, traveling with his household, which included his wife Céleste, a few servants, and personal belongings.

Ultimately, Chateaubriand's dire situation in 1817, the year following his dismissal, proved pivotal to his subsequent development. During that year of despair, two events changed the course of his life. The first life-changing event was a dinner at the home of Madame Germaine de Staël in late May, where he renewed his acquaintance with Juliette Récamier, who would become his muse, confidante, and companion for the remainder of their long lives. Madame Récamier was not only beautiful, graceful, and charming but also well-read, thoughtful, and witty. We can sense her presence today through two portraits of her, among the most famous in the history of French art, one by Jacques-Louis David in 1800 (see figure 2) and the other by his student François Gerard in 1802. Seated between Chateaubriand and Madame Récamier at dinner that evening was a young American scholar named George Ticknor, who, preparing to assume a professorship at Harvard, showed a keen interest in meeting them.

In his diary, Ticknor commented on Juliette:

Madame Récamier must now be forty or more...and the lustre of that beauty which filled Europe with its fame has certainly faded. I do not mean to say she is not still beautiful, for she certainly is, and very beautiful. Her figure is fine, her mild eyes full of expression, and her arm and hand most beautiful...her conversation gay and full of vivacity...always without extravagance.[11]

Ticknor continued with a description of Chateaubriand:

Chateaubriand is a short man, with a dark complexion, black hair, black eyes, and altogether a most marked countenance. It needs no skill in physiognomy, to say that he is at once a man of firmness and decision of character, for every feature and every movement of his person announce it. He gives...a grave and serious turn to the conversation in which he engages....His conversation, like his character, seems prompt, original, decisive, and, like his works, full of sparkling phrases, happy combinations and thoughts, sometimes more brilliant than just. His general tone was declamatory, though not extravagantly so, and its general effect that of interesting the feelings and attention, without producing conviction or changing opinion.[12]

The second life-changing event that year for Chateaubriand occurred in late July while he and Céleste were guests at the castle of Baron Montboissier in the Loire Valley. While resting in a wood, enthralled by the song of a wood thrush, Chateaubriand was suddenly overcome by reminiscence of his youth and resolved to devote his attention to his memoirs, which were to become his most enduring legacy. He described the moment:

I was roused from my reflections by the warbling of a thrush perched on the highest branch of a birch. This magic sound brought my father's lands back before my eyes in an instant....The bird's song in the woods of Combourg spoke to me of a bliss I was sure I would attain; the same song in the park here at Montboissier reminds me of the days I have lost in pursuit of that old, elusive bliss. There is nothing more for me to learn....Let me profit from the few moments that remain to me; let me hasten to describe my youth while I can still recall it. A sailor, leaving his enchanted island forever, writes his journal in sight of the land as it slowly slips away. It is a land that will soon be lost.[13]

By 1820, Chateaubriand had again begun to publish pieces in support of the reign of King Louis XVIII and shortly thereafter was reappointed by the government. He returned to London in April 1822 as French ambassador to the Court of St. James's. During his summer there, he was well known among the English aristocracy for his lavish receptions, for which his personal chef, the legendary Montmireil, devised the beef dish that to this day carries his name— chateaubriand steak. Chateaubriand left London in September 1822, having been dispatched to the Congress of Verona. He lost his influence over government policy after championing a military campaign to reestablish the Spanish Bourbons that depleted the French treasury, though its principal purpose, from Chateaubriand's point of view, was to increase French prestige, an objective it met.

Quitting government service in 1830, Chateaubriand devoted the rest of his life to writing his memoirs. Céleste died in 1846, whereupon he proposed to Juliette Récamier, who laughingly reminded him that at their age marriage would be foolish nonsense. He died on July 4, 1848, two months shy of his eightieth birthday. Before she died, less than a year later, Juliette assisted in delivering his manuscript to a newspaper for publication. Ultimately, his extraordinary lengthy memoirs, which he had ordered not to be published until after his death, were published serially in the newspaper beginning in 1850, under the provocative title *Mémoires d'outre-tombe (Memoirs from Beyond the Grave)*.

More than a decade before his death Chateaubriand secured an agreement with the civic leadership of Saint-Malo to ensure that his grave would be located on the side of a prominent hill in the center of the bay that marks the historic city—an island called Le Grand Bé. It is accessible by foot only at low tide for ninety minutes, the sole grave on that small island, marked by a Celtic cross hewn from local stone, and with his underground remains facing his longtime friend, the eternal sea. Chateaubriand specified that there be no indication of the occupant of the grave or description, just a simple cross (see figure 3). Even so, on the wall facing the sea the city council later placed a plaque with these words: "A great French writer wanted to rest here in order to hear only the sea and the wind. Passersby, please respect his last wish."[14]

Chateaubriand's personal, often melancholic, bold tales, released at the dawn of European romanticism, captured the French imagination. His novella *René* became so influential that it was detached from *The Genius of Christianity* and published on its own in 1805 and again, to raise funds, in the fateful year 1817, along with *Atala* in a longer narrative set in America, *Les Natchez*. *René* seemed to capture perfectly the wayward emotions of young people living in those tumultuous times. Its impact on French audiences paralleled the effect Goethe's *Sorrows of Young Werther* had had on the preceding generation of German readers.

Chateaubriand was not a literary craftsman or a scholar concerned with detail. His fanciful plots could not be taken seriously, nor were his characters well developed or persuasively capable of purposeful action. Occasionally his essays and travel descriptions contained errors and borrowings from others, verging on plagiarism. What makes his work memorable and powerfully influential is how his seemingly effortless but often startling combinations of words pull readers into his narrative through a continually inventive display of dazzling style. As one of his biographers, Friedrich Sieburg, put it, "It could be said that the language itself was astonished at its own capacity."[15] Chateaubriand's gripping memoirs brilliantly deployed a fluidity of time, in which he wrote from the present to the past, often inserting commentary by his mature self into musings about his youthful one. His fecund source of inspiration was his narcissistic obsession with himself. In effect, Chateaubriand succeeded in making his life itself a work of art.

Marcel Proust claimed that his own masterpiece *In Search of Lost Time*, launched by the memory of tasting a pastry, was inspired by Chateaubriand's memoirs, which were themselves inspired by the memory of a birdcall. Chateaubriand's writings, regarded as the starting point for modern French aestheticism, became a beacon to many writers besides Proust, including Victor Hugo and Charles Baudelaire. Indeed, traces of Chateaubriand's enduring artistic legacy can be found in many subsequent cultural movements in France, including naturalism, surrealism, and existentialism.

A great artist finds a way to touch others by producing works that resonate with truths they feel within themselves. The magic François-René Chateaubriand conjures with breathtakingly affecting language in his memoirs reveals an essentially human spirit generating themes that those who engage his storytelling can recognize. In the life he portrayed for us I detected echoes in my own family over generations: the capacity of education to enable and amplify positive life trajectories; the value of pursuing creative expression and intellectual inquiry; the joy of adventurous exploration in the New World and other distant lands; the experience of exile and emigration as a means for insight into the human condition; fascination with the sea as a reminder of the eternity from which we evolved, and as a source of liberation and discovery, infinitely connected, as it is, to every land mass we inhabit; investigation of religion as a means of self-discovery; and service to state and society for the benefit of humankind.

So resonant were aspects of my ancestors' lives with those portrayed by Chateaubriand that I fully expected to find in his writing some elucidation of the mystery surrounding the girl named Mary who figured prominently in my family story. What I found initially were details illuminating Chateaubriand's fascinating perspective on love and women. Based on surviving letters, reports in public documents about him, and occasional reflections in his memoirs, I learned that Chateaubriand was proud of having secured the affections of numerous women, especially prominent society icons, and of his charms as a great lover. At the same time, he remained tied in a marriage devoid of physical intimacy with his lifelong wife, Céleste. Though he maintained that his respect for Catholic ritual demanded such bondage, the sins of his perpetual adultery were no impediment to their continuation. Even so, Chateaubriand and Céleste's domestic arrangement appeared to work for them. He was described by others as unfailingly gracious to and respectful of her, and he trusted her with managing the household affairs. For her part, she insisted on maintaining the artifice of their marriage and being known as Madame Chateaubriand, but did not conceal her resentment of her unusual relationship with him, customarily letting others know about her refusal to read his literary works and commenting disparagingly to friends about his behavior, often resorting to sarcastic comments about her husband's "ladies."

Chateaubriand's love affairs, while intense, were frequently brief, with one ending abruptly just as another began. Although seemingly a recipe for bitterness on the part of his abandoned mistresses, rather than begrudging his departure they seemed to expect it as part of their surrender to him. In fact, many of his lovers—whether seeking him, with him, or dropped by him— unabashedly confessed they were crazy about him. Certainly, some of his relationships were transactional, with his lover in some way furthering his career, but his behavior, while seemingly capricious, was not uncaring. On at least one occasion, upon learning of the grave illness of a former lover he rushed to her bedside, holding her hand tenderly and whispering to her as she died.

Because Chateaubriand's life since childhood had been forged in feminine sensibility—surrounded, as he was, by the omnipresence of his caring sisters—he had a special capacity for understanding women, even though his many intimate exploits suggest he was incapable of engaging with a woman in a lasting loving monogamous relationship. It was as if his imaginary Sylphide, his feminine ideal, was always just beyond his reach; no mere mortal lover could fulfill what his fantasy had created. Throughout his life, he was surely in love with the idea of love.

As Chateaubriand began to shape his immortality in his memoirs, he avoided much mention of his consorts, focusing instead on the power of his imaginary Sylphide and on his flirtatious romance with Charlotte Ives. Then late in life, together with Madame Récamier, he burned love letters he had received, along with other correspondence he chose to hide from posterity. It is likely that any letters he may have received from my ancestors Mary and her son Thomas were also destroyed along the way.

Of special interest to me was the role Mary played in Chateaubriand's life, in particular how they related to one another during her adolescence and his years in London. Following his war experience, subsequent illness on the isle of Jersey, and first desperate months on English soil, his love life was likely very quiet. Mary, as a young girl, may have been the first female friend with whom he became acquainted in England. Charlotte, also young, may have been the second. His encounters with both young women occurred in his mid-twenties, when he was exiled and lonely. In his memoirs, Chateaubriand romanticized his feelings for Charlotte without implying a sexual encounter. But what could have been his relationship with Mary? In my journey to understand how the life of Chateaubriand intersected with the lives of my ancestors, I next turned my attention to Mary.

Figure 1. Portrait of François-Réne de Chateaubriand, shown meditating on the ruins of Rome, by Anne-Louis Girodet de Roussy-Trioson (1808). Reproduced by permission of Saint-Malo Musée d'Histoire.

Figure 2. Portrait of Madame Juliette Récamier by Jacques-Louis David (1800). Reproduced by permission of RMN Grand Palais /Art Resource, New York.

Figure 3. Tomb of Chateaubriand on the island of Le Grand Bé in the Gulf of Saint-Malo, facing the Celtic Sea. Photograph by Daniel Fallon.

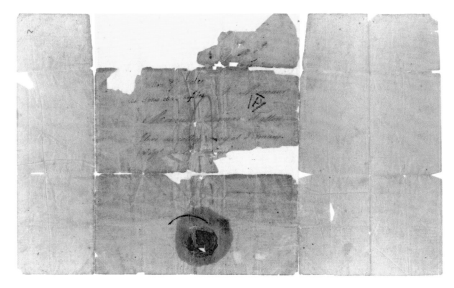

Figure 4. Envelope addressed to Monsieur Thomas Fallon containing letter from Chateaubriand, dated June 28, 1817. Courtesy of Daniel Fallon.

Figure 5. Letter to Thomas Fallon from Chateaubriand, dated June 28, 1817. Courtesy of Daniel Fallon.

Ce n'est que ce matin Monsieur, que j'ai appris
que M. le Vicomte de Chateaubriand vous accordait
la permission que je lui ai demandée pour vous
d'aller passer les vacances chez les parents de
deux de vos camarades. J'espère qu'il est encore
temps de profiter de cette permission. Je suis fâché
de n'avoir pu vous l'annoncer plutôt. Je vous
souhaite toutes sortes d'agrément.

J'ai l'honneur d'être, Monsieur, votre très humble et
très obéissant serviteur

Hyacinthe Pilorge

Paris le 20 Août 1817

P.S. Pour que cela ne souffre aucune difficulté je
fais part de cette permission, par le même courrier,
à M. le Proviseur du Collège

Figure 6. Letter to Thomas Fallon from Hyacinthe Pilorge, dated August 20, 1817. Courtesy of Daniel Fallon.

Marriages in March 1799

136 Patrick Fallon of St Mary le bone a Bachelor and Mary Eliza Neale of this Parish Spinster were married in this Church by Licence this Ninth Day of March in the Year 1799 by me

This Marriage was solemnized between us { Patrick Fallon / Mary Eliza Neale

In the presence of { Hugh Kelly / Sarah West / Barbara Bargrove

137 Thomas Smith and Martha Ballard both of this Parish were married in

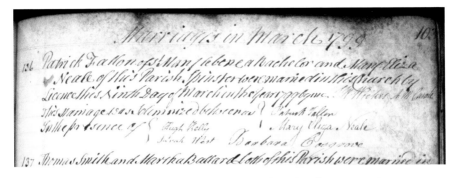

Figure 7.1. Marriage register, St. George's Church of Hanover Square, March 9, 1799, listing for Mary Neale and Patrick Fallon. Photograph by Daniel Fallon.

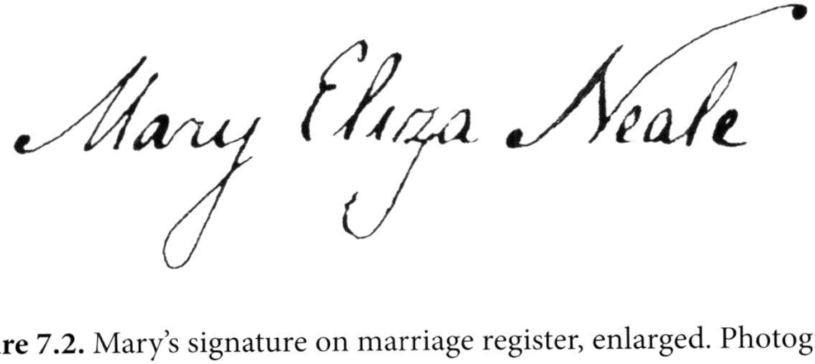

Figure 7.2. Mary's signature on marriage register, enlarged. Photograph by Daniel Fallon.

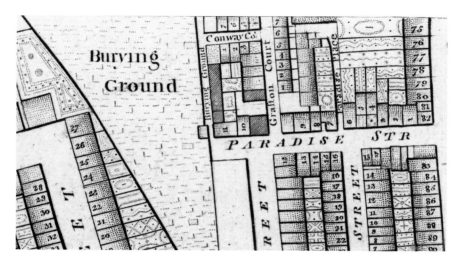

Figure 8. Detail from Richard Horwood's map of London, showing No. 10 Paradise Street (January 1794). Courtesy of Westminster City Archives, London.

Figure 9. Portrait of Thomas Fallon, perhaps age twenty-two (c. 1822); artist unknown. Courtesy of Daniel Fallon.

Figure 10. Portrait of Thomas Fallon in Colombia, perhaps age forty-five (c. 1845); artist unknown. Courtesy of Marcela Samper de Angel.

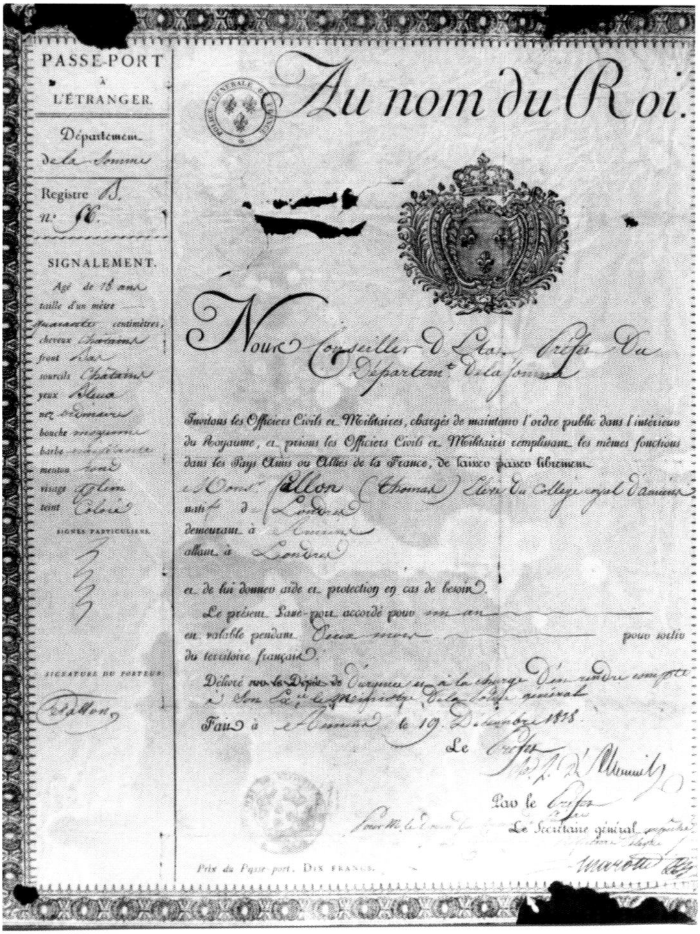
PASSE-PORT
À
L'ÉTRANGER.
Département de la Somme
Registre
n°
SIGNALEMENT.
Agé de 18 ans
taille d'un mètre
centimètres,
cheveux
front
sourcils châtains
yeux bleus
nez ordinaire
bouche
barbe
menton rond
visage
teint coloré
SIGNES PARTICULIERS.
SIGNATURE DU PORTEUR.
Fallon

Au nom du Roi.

Nous Conseiller d'État Préfet du Département de la Somme

Invitons les Officiers Civils et Militaires, chargés de maintenir l'ordre public dans l'intérieur du Royaume, et prions les Officiers Civils et Militaires remplissant les mêmes fonctions dans les Pays Amis ou Alliés de la France, de laisser passer librement
M. Fallon (Thomas) Élève du Collège royal d'Amiens
natif de Londres
demeurant à Amiens
allant à Londres
et de lui donner aide et protection en cas de besoin.
Le présent Passe-port accordé pour un an
est valable pendant deux mois pour sortir du territoire français.
Délivré
Fait à Amiens le 19 Décembre 1818.
Le Préfet
Par le Préfet
Le Secrétaire général
Prix du Passe-port. DIX FRANCS.

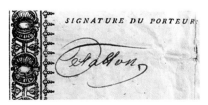

Figure 11.1. Thomas Fallon's passport (1818). Courtesy of Pablo Quijano-Samper.

SIGNATURE DU PORTEUR:
Fallon

Figure 11.2. Thomas's signature on passport, enlarged. Courtesy of Pablo Quijano-Samper.

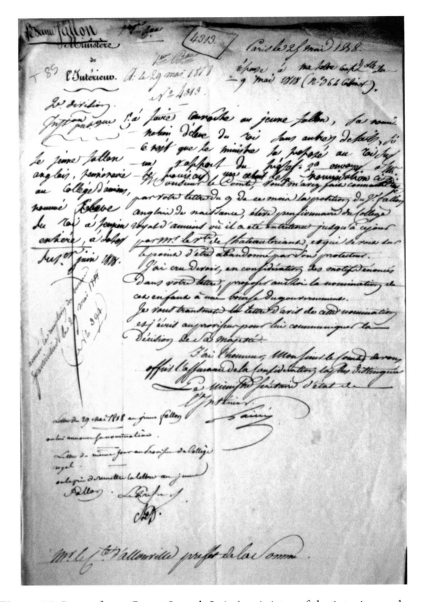

Figure 12. Letter from Count Joseph Lainé, minister of the interior under King Louis XVIII, to Count Alexandre Louis d'Allonville, prefect of the Département de la Somme, with notes from the prefect, awarding scholarship to "the young Fallon," dated May 29, 1818. Photograph by Daniel Fallon.

Figure 13. Pencil sketch of Cornelia Fallon, by her brother, Diego Fallon (1858). Courtesy of Daniel Fallon.

Figure 14. Image of Diego Fallon on Colombian commemorative stamp issued October 1, 1984. Courtesy of Daniel Fallon.

Figure 15. Photograph of Diego Fallon family (c. 1885). Back row (left to right): Diego, Luís Tomás, Cornelia; front row (left to right): Diego José, Amalia, María. Courtesy of Daniel Fallon.

Figure 16. Photograph of Carlos Fallon at sea, perhaps age twenty (1929).
Courtesy of Daniel Fallon.

CHAPTER 3

Pursuing the Mystery
of Mary

MYSTERY MOTIVATES.

London at the end of the eighteenth century was home to Mary and Patrick while Chateaubriand was there in exile; that was the bedrock of our family story. As my nagging curiosity pushed me to comb through whatever additional family archives I could find, none revealed any physical evidence of Mary or Patrick. The two were characters in an oral family history that was durable and persuasive, but not substantiated enough to convince skeptics of their physical existence. To find such evidence, I would have to search more deeply through records of the period, and to better understand their life circumstances I would have to consider conditions in London more than two centuries ago.

In 1790, London had become by far the largest city in Europe, roughly twice the size of Paris, four times the size of Vienna, and five times the size of each of the next three largest cities. By 1800, it had even surpassed Beijing to become the biggest city in the world. Londoners of that time shared their city with horses, the only relief from walking as a means of transport. Richard Horwood's detailed maps of the city show horse-care facilities appearing every three or four blocks along mostly cobblestone streets. In our twenty-first-century world, we have become inured to noise pollution: jackhammers, aircraft, internal combustion engines, sirens, automobile horns, acoustic amplification, and more. At the end of the eighteenth century, Londoners had it better. The loudest sounds a typical resident would ever hear were the tread of horse hooves on the street, tumbling carriage wheels, the barking of a dog, the whinny of a horse, the cries of a street peddler, or an occasional clap of thunder.

Sanitation was irregular, with trash often discarded on the street, along with uncaught droppings from horses, washed away from time to time by storms. Refuse and animal excretions wafted aromas as familiar as they were unwelcome. Darkness at night kept most people off the streets, in the safety of their homes. There were dim streetlamps in some populated areas, fueled by oil and lit by lamplighters, but only reliably available during the darkest winter months. Most citizens needing to go somewhere at night would hire a boy with a flaming torch to light the way and scare off lurking muggers. For as many as sixty days each year, London fog settled through temperature inversions in the low-lying basin the city occupied not far from the sea, mingling with the smoke from wood- and coal-burning fireplaces of densely compacted lodgings and shops, making the air acrid and visibility poor. On foggy evenings, it was rare to see more than six feet ahead.

It was in this city at this time that I sought to discover the missing puzzle pieces describing the relationship between

Chateaubriand and the Irish girl Mary O'Neill, whose charming story had been faithfully passed down through successive generations in my family. The crumbling letters to Mary's son Thomas from Chateaubriand that my father had left me offered a portal of entry. I took the envelopes with their remains to a document preservation specialist and had them reassembled and placed in clear protective sleeves to prevent further deterioration. When the task was finished, there were two complete letters, the first with an accompanying envelope that read (see figure 4 for the original version):

To
Mister Thomas Fallon
Pupil at the Royal College of Amiens
Department of the Somme

I asked a scholar of French literature to translate the letters into English. He was astonished to see at the end of the first letter Viscount Chateaubriand's distinctive signature, a capital *C* in an elegant swirl. The handwriting in the letter was not like the signature, revealing that the letter had been written by a secretary taking dictation and then signed in affectionate shorthand by the viscount (see figure 5 for the original version):

Paris. June 28, 1817

I send you, my little friend, a package containing:

a blue coat
two pairs of cloth pants
a black pair of short pants
a pair of nankeen short pants
two white quilted vests

It will be necessary to have these fitted to your size. I have thus sent to your Director the sum of 30f to pay for the alterations. I have also sent him notice of the package.

Continue your studies as ever, my dear fallon, and count on my friendship.

deCh[1]

The second letter had been written and signed by Chateaubriand's secretary, a gentleman named Hyacinthe Pilorge (see figure 6 for the original version):

It was only this morning, sir, that I learned that the Viscount Chateaubriand has given you permission that I had asked of him to allow you to spend the vacation at the home of the parents of your two friends. I hope there is still time for you to take advantage of this permission. I am sorry not to have been able to inform you of it sooner. I hope you will enjoy yourself thoroughly.

I have the honor of being, sir, your most humble and obliging servant.

Hyacinthe Pilorge

Paris. August 20, 1817

P.S. So that you will encounter no difficulties, I have informed the Director of your school of the Viscount's permission by this same mail.[2]

These letters, unknown to Chateaubriand scholars and unique to my family, show Chateaubriand as a caring benefactor genuinely concerned for Thomas's welfare. The second letter further indicates that Chateaubriand viewed himself as at least the temporary guardian of the boy, taking responsibility for providing school authorities with the necessary permission for Thomas to leave the school premises during vacations. My family story recounts that Chateaubriand assumed this duty in gratitude to the boy's mother, Mary, for having helped him when he was destitute, banishing the specter of death in his first year of exile in London. For Chateaubriand, this was no minor act of beneficence, especially in 1817, when he was in financial distress and declaring bankruptcy. I wondered if there could be other reasons Chateaubriand had assumed responsibility for Thomas's education and well-being in France. To find out more, I needed to dig deeper.

I was encouraged upon discovering, among my father's sketchy notes on the subject, references to a biography, *Chateaubriand* by Joan Evans, published in 1939 by Macmillan of London, along with a Library of Congress call number and some scribbles, including the word *mistress*. I located the book. When Chateaubriand returned to Paris in 1800, Evans writes, he "earned his living by contributing pot-boiling articles on literary criticism to Fontanes' papers. Out of his scanty funds he paid a regular allowance to a mistress: first to an Englishwoman named Fallon, and then to a succession of Frenchwomen who were part of the journalists' world of the day."[3]

Later in her book, Evans confirms that in 1817, having lost his government position, Chateaubriand became financially distressed, stopping payment on his debts, but that "the school fees of the son of his first mistress, Mrs. Fallon, were regularly paid."[4] I was astonished that Evans was implying the guileless girl of our family stories, Mary O'Neill—my great-great-great-grandmother—was Chateaubriand's mistress, and that my New World forebears and I were not Fallons, after all, but actually Chateaubriands! My father had apparently chosen to omit Evans's suppositions from his retellings of the family story. His own father, my grandfather, had adamantly rejected any implication of romance between Mary and the famous Frenchman, insisting that the only relationship was of a kindhearted innocent schoolgirl helping a refined gentleman in distress. Our family's remembrance of Mary O'Neill cast no shadow on Chateaubriand's character. My father had obviously relied on firmly established family tradition, ignoring the speculative view offered by Joan Evans.

Although my family's story was uncomplicated, I was now aware that the circumstances it described could harbor concealed meaning. Perhaps Chateaubriand had been closer to Mary than the tale had implied. Could he have imagined that Thomas was his own son? And if so, how would I rethink my ancestry and inform my many relatives descended from Thomas Fallon?

Certainly, Chateaubriand was prone to letting his heart lead him into intimate relationships with women, both young and worldly, with whom he discerned or created a shared attraction. He described some affairs of the heart in his memoirs, while others are documented in letters he wrote or received. His relationships with at least fifteen women are well known, including some of the most prominent of his time: Henriette de Belloy, Pauline de Beaumont, Delphine de Custine, Natalie de Noailles, Claire de Duras, Françoise-Fanny Bail, Juliette Récamier, Frédérique de Cumberland, Emilie Lafond, Jeanne-Emilie Leverd, Cordelia de Castellane, Fortunée Hamelin, Hortense Allart, Marie-Amélie de Vichet, and Léontine de Villeneuve.[5] His liaisons with a few of these women were likely platonic; for instance, some scholars suspect that his decades-long close friendship with Juliette Récamier was never physically intimate. Others were more obviously affairs of heart, soul, and flesh.

Questions about the paternity of an ancestor can stir one to action, and it certainly did in my case. First I wrote to Macmillan, asking if Joan Evans's research papers were available. Next I wrote to the archivist at Amiens, France, inquiring about records at the school. It seemed from its tone and content that the letter Chateaubriand had written to my great-great-grandfather, Thomas Fallon, might have been directed to a boy perhaps as young as fourteen. And if the boy was that age in 1817, he would have been born in 1803 and therefore Chateaubriand, in Rome at the time, could not have been his father. I also wrote to the Association of Genealogists and Record Agents in London and received back a list of certified English genealogists. I chose one who specialized in late-eighteenth- and early-nineteenth-century London, Mr. Edward J. Lowe of Bromley, Kent, and commissioned him to conduct a search of records relating to Mary O'Neill, Patrick Fallon, and Thomas Fallon.

Shortly after sending off the first flurry of letters, I came across a biography of Chateaubriand by George D. Painter, published in 1979. I marveled at the author's detailed scholarship but was disappointed to discover that the book was subtitled *Volume I* and ended with Chateaubriand's arrival in England in 1793, omitting the last fifty-five years of his life. Even though a three-volume biography had been projected, the latter two volumes were never completed. Mr. Painter had enjoyed a distinguished career as incunabulist for the British Museum. Upon retiring from that position, he resumed his lifelong devotion to French literature, publishing what is regarded as the definitive biography of Marcel Proust, the second volume of which won a major prize, and later an expanded and revised version of his earlier biography of André Gide. He then turned his attention to Chateaubriand, whereupon his initial volume also won a major prize. After learning that Mr. Painter, born in 1914, was still active, I wrote to him at his seaside home on the coast of England, asking what he might know of the relationship between Thomas Fallon and Chateaubriand.

I then directed my attention to the viscount himself as a resource. It was obvious to me that Mary and her son Thomas were unusually significant people in Chateaubriand's life. After all, Joan Evans reported transfers of funds to Mrs. Fallon in 1800 and my letters confirmed that Chateaubriand was supporting Thomas in 1817—two years in which he had scant income and few if any financial reserves. If his interest in Mary and Thomas was purely philanthropic, there would be no reason for him to hide his sponsorship of the boy. Since he was a dedicated memoirist, I concluded, then somewhere in his extensive recollections he must have touched upon the impactful relationship he had with Mary and Thomas. Surely, in memoirs scheduled for publication after his death he would mention something about these two people. I decided to comb through the memoirs once more, searching meticulously for any possible reference to them.

My fastidious search bore no obvious fruit, which confounded me. Chateaubriand, obsessed with his own character to the extent of writing forty-two volumes of memoir over decades and scheduling them for posthumous publication, had made no mention of any relationship with Mary or Thomas! Yet Chateaubriand was known to enjoy occasional philanthropy, providing assistance to family members and others, both financially and through the influence he had acquired, and was not shy about public acknowledgment of these gifts. Clearly, it seemed to me, a significant relationship between Chateaubriand and my ancestors Mary and Thomas was willfully hidden from both his private and public records. This frustrating dissonance increased the urgency of my need to know the facts. I was determined to enter the strange world of long-gone people; seek whatever they might have left behind; and hope to discover, perhaps through a tangle of motives, some comprehensible explanation for Chateaubriand's silence about his relations with Mary and Thomas. I had stumbled on a worthy mystery, one soon to become the cornerstone of my quest.

It then occurred to me that one brief entry in Chateaubriand's memoirs might have been a link, although it seemed unlikely because it contained a different spelling of Mary's surname and the time did not correspond with any element in my family story. The entry described an incident in London in early 1798, a little more than a year after Chateaubriand had returned there from his sojourn in Beccles and Bungay. He wrote:

> I settled myself in the Hampstead Road. Here I lodged for some months in the house of a Mrs. O'Leary, an Irish widow....Mrs. O'Leary's visitors were old neighbors, with whom I was obliged to take tea in the old fashion. Madame de Staël has described this scene in Corinne, at the house of Lady Engermond: "My dear, do you think the water boils well enough to make the tea?"—"My dear, I think it is a little too soon." There came also to these tea-parties a tall, beautiful, young Irish woman, Mary Neale, under the escort of a guardian. She discerned some heart-wound as she looked deeply into my eyes, for she said to me: "You carry your heart in a sling." I carried my heart I know not how.[6]

The description of this encounter occupied just three sentences in the lengthy memoirs, after which Chateaubriand changed the subject tersely. Could Chateaubriand's Mary Neale be the Mary O'Neill of my family stories? I wondered. Latin Americans tend to place the letter *O* in front of every name they believe is Irish, and, since my family story had been transmitted orally, the spelling of the Irish girl's name could have taken any form, I told myself. Imagining an audible *O* placed in front of *Neale*, it is easy to assume that my family actually carried the famous royal Irish appellation "O'Neill." But, I reminded myself, the Mary Neale of Chateaubriand's description was clearly not a twelve-year-old girl he met in a park; nor was he living in her house. My faith in the family story began to waver, for I had found no historical record of a Mary O'Neill or a Patrick Fallon.

Meanwhile, I received a letter from Evans's publisher, Macmillan, informing me that I was referring to Dame Joan Evans—Fellow of St. Hugh's College, Oxford University, author of more than a dozen books, one of the most widely published historians of the twentieth century, who had died in 1977—and that although her editors had retained their correspondence with Dame Evans, they did not have her research records. The publisher suggested I write to Oxford University.

Subsequently, I wrote to Oxford University and received a reply stating that no records associated with Dame Evans had been found there. I met with a similar lack of success when approaching other suggested sources, such as the Society of Antiquaries of London and the literary executors of Dame Evans's estate. I also learned from eminent historians that Dame Evans had been notorious for habitually publishing startling claims and refusing to divulge her sources. If her allegation about Chateaubriand's 1800 payment was to be believed, I reasoned, she had most likely consulted bankers' records, which were relatively available in Paris at that time; found a transfer of payment from Chateaubriand to a Mrs. Fallon; knew about the tuition payment for Thomas Fallon in 1817; and drew what appeared to be a logical conclusion. If such a financial transaction happened, it is possible that Chateaubriand was occasionally sending small monetary gifts to Mary around 1800, perhaps in celebration of the birth of her first child—transfers that had to have been international since Mary was at home with Patrick and Thomas in London.

I next received a series of letters from the Amiens archivist. At first, her tone seemed promising as she described contacting the school authorities. In the end, however, she reported the disappointing news that the school's records had all been destroyed in 1940 when German troops had bombarded Amiens while marching through the city during World War II.

Then I heard from Mr. Lowe, the genealogist. I knew that locating a birth record for Thomas Fallon would be a difficult challenge. After all, the Fallons were Irish Catholics in London at a time when Catholicism was suppressed and the Irish were generally unwelcome. Mr. Lowe, it turned out, was indeed unable to locate the birth record because, as he noted, an easing of prohibitions against Catholic places of worship and Catholic schools did not begin until passage of the Roman Catholic Relief Act of 1791, an invitation to tolerance that resulted in noticeable societal benefits only after many years. Catholics had by then become adept at observing their religion in private. Religious records, if they existed, would not likely have survived; and civil registration of births, deaths, and marriages was not begun in England until 1837.

Mr. Lowe went on to say that for marriages to be legally recognized after passage of the Marriage Act of 1753, they had to take place in the Church of England, even the marriages of Catholics and other so-called nonconformists. Only marriages of Jews and Quakers, Scottish marriages, and marriages of the royal family were exempt from this ruling. Thus, for the marriage of a Catholic to be recognized by civil law, a ceremony had to be performed by an Anglican priest in an Anglican church, where careful records were kept. The Marriage Act thus spawned a trove of Anglican Church records for a genealogist to search. It was there that Mr. Lowe succeeded in locating the marriage record of Patrick and Mary.

The event was recorded in the register of St. George's Church of Hanover Square, a quite fashionable corner of London then and now. This church had earlier been the religious home of the faithful parishioner George Friedrich Handel and had become one of the most popular churches in London for marriages, especially of the elite, including King George III's sixth son, Prince Augustus Frederick, to Lady Augusta Murray on December 5, 1793. Percy Bysshe Shelley was also married there—to his first wife, Harriet Westbrook, on March 24, 1814, after returning from their elopement to Scotland three years earlier.

The Anglican curate T. W. Wickes had recorded in the register of St. George's Church of Hanover Square: "Patrick Fallon of St Marylebone a Bachelor and Mary Eliza Neale of this Parish Spinster were married in this Church by license this Ninth Day of March in the Year 1799 by me." Later, during a trip to London, I located the book in the Westminster Archives and photographed the page with the entry, including signatures of the wedding couple and their witnesses. From this document, I was able to confirm that Mary's family name was indeed "Neale," exactly as Chateaubriand had spelled it in his memoirs when describing his encounter at Mrs. O'Leary's tea party with the young Irish woman a year before her wedding. Her signature, complete with her middle name—Mary Eliza Neale—is elegant, in a learned copperplate (see figures 7.1 and 7.2), indicating that she had benefited from an excellent education. This concrete evidence of the marriage of Mary and Patrick established not only their existence but also details about their lives that were new to those of us who had heard my father's family stories.

When I finally obtained a copy of the marriage license, I saw that Patrick had listed his occupation as "hatter" and had been of sufficient standing to provide security for a bond of £200, considered a fortune at the time. There were other odd surprises. The license had been issued by the vicar general of the archbishop of Canterbury, the second highest ecclesiastical authority in the kingdom, who did not usually bother with ordinary marriage licenses. Finally, a marriage license was not necessary if the bride was a resident of the parish where the wedding was to occur, yet the officiating curate had noted in his register that Mary was "of this parish."

The usual reason couples sought a license was to marry immediately, since a license would legally allow them to circumvent the otherwise required calling of the banns, a public announcement of an impending marriage, which took three consecutive Sundays. The marriage license for Mary and Patrick had been issued on Thursday, March 7, 1799, and the wedding was on Saturday, March 9, 1799. Since the wedding had proceeded almost immediately upon issuance of the license, it would seem that the need for an official civil ceremony had been urgent. Had Mary been in a predicament?

If Mary were pregnant as she stood at the wedding altar with her bridegroom, it would not have been unusual. A remarkable sexual revolution had taken place in England during the previous decades. By the middle of the eighteenth century, profound changes in sexual behavior were well underway.[7] The last case of a person criminally punished in England for consensual heterosexual relations out of wedlock occurred in 1746. Racy pamphlets and pictorial works, such as William Hogarth's series of paintings and engravings titled *A Harlot's Progress*, began to proliferate in the first half of the eighteenth century. Then a new art form, the novel, appeared, and as these works of narrative fiction began to command public favor, erotic allusions sprouted occasionally from their pages.

The first decidedly erotic novel published in English was *Memoirs of a Woman of Pleasure*, known popularly by the name of its protagonist, Fanny Hill. It was produced in London in 1748 and promptly banned by courts as criminally pornographic, a restriction upheld on both sides of the Atlantic until the mid-twentieth century. While the novel was officially suppressed, innumerable contraband copies in multiple editions remained in wide circulation Similar relaxation of sexual restrictions occurred throughout Europe during the eighteenth century, and by 1782, the well-known French erotic novel *Les Liaisons Dangereuses* was published.

The rapidity of the sexual revolution of the eighteenth century was striking, especially since, around 1650, only a hundred years before the publication of London's first erotic novel, sexual norms in general English society had been highly conservative. This earlier period was dominated by the turbulent clashes of the Oliver Cromwell years, which resulted in the beheading of the English King Charles I and bitter struggles between Puritans, Anglicans, Presbyterians, and Catholics over the establishment of a national religion. The then prevailing modesty between the sexes resulted in such low fertility rates that the English population fell below its replacement rate by the end of the century.

Historical demographers have established that in the 1670s about 1 percent of all first births in England were illegitimate, but by the 1790s about 25 percent of all first births were out of wedlock and an additional 25 percent were associated with mothers pregnant at the time of marriage. Over this period of time, the mean age of women getting married also fell dramatically and included a substantial number of teenage brides. Even though the legal age of majority was twenty-one, the age usually required to obtain a marriage license, it was common for younger women seeking marriage to assert that they were at least twenty-one. The radical changes in sexual behavior over the eighteenth century also caused fertility rates to increase by more than 60 percent, making England one of the fastest-growing countries in Europe.[8] Therefore, if my adventurous great-great-great-grandmother, Mary Eliza Neale, had been pregnant at the time of her marriage in 1799, it would hardly have been cause for devastating scandal. All the same, a prompt marriage would have been considered prudent.

While contemplating the discovery of Mary's wedding record, I received from Mr. Painter, Chateaubriand's biographer, an extraordinary letter carefully typewritten on ten pages of lightweight blue overseas correspondence stationery. He had located his notes on the name Fallon and placed as much of the information as he could in the context of his Chateaubriand research. He informed me that in 1922 a scholar named Maurice Levaillant had published a book, revised in 1948, based on letters he had recently discovered from Chateaubriand to an elderly confidant, Jean-Baptiste Le Moine, who served as a financial secretary. Chronicled in Levaillant's book was a letter dated July 1817—exactly a month between the two letters in my possession—from Chateaubriand to Le Moine, containing a long list of instructions, one of which was: "I have always forgotten to ask you whether you have received the receipt from the headmaster at the Amiens School. If you haven't received it, ask for it and let him know at the same time that I am quite agreeable to the young man spending his holidays at one of his school friends' homes."[9] When Levaillant discovered this instruction, around 1920, school records were still intact in Amiens. Puzzled by the revelation that Chateaubriand, while bankrupt, would be paying expenses for a student, Levaillant had made a beeline for the school in Amiens and determined that the name of the young man was Thomas Fallon. It was clearly from this source that Dame Joan Evans had learned of the 1817 tuition payment for a boy named Fallon.

In addition to Levaillant's discovery that Chateaubriand had paid the tuition and fees for Thomas Fallon in 1817, Painter relayed other important information about the Frenchman. Included was a copy of an essay Painter had recently published in an English journal, describing his painstaking research on Chateaubriand's lodgings in London during his first year in exile, 1793. The essay was intended to be the first chapter in the second volume of Painter's projected three-volume biography of Chateaubriand, a work he was unable to complete before his death in 2005 at age ninety-one.

Painter's essay reminds the reader that during Chateaubriand's early months of exile in London he had often been forced to move. After nearly starving and subsequently rescuing his friend Hingant from attempted suicide, Chateaubriand had moved again in fall 1793 to an attic room he described as follows: "My friends…soon installed me in the vicinity of Marylebone Street, in a garret with a skylight overlooking a cemetery. Every night the watchman's rattle told me that someone had come to rob the cadavers."[10]

Painter wrote:

It is curious that no one has identified the whereabouts of this new lodging, although, as with the "garret in Holburn," one has only to follow his exact directions. It was, he says, "in the neighborhood of Marylebone Street"— that is, the modern Marylebone High Street, which was then so called—"in a garret with a skylight overlooking a cemetery"; and, by a dramatic contrast which impressed him twenty-nine years later, in 1822, when he returned to London in his glory as French Ambassador, it lay "opposite to" or "facing" his own magnificent embassy in Portland Place. The cemetery, the only one in the entire district, was at the end of Paradise Street (the modern Moxon Street) only a few yards west of Marylebone High Street; one can see it in Horwood's contemporary atlas of London in the 1790s, and even walk in it to this day, for it is now a public recreation ground. Paradise or Moxon Street still opens opposite the western end of Weymouth Street, which runs straight into Portland Place. The French Embassy in 1822 was at 51 Portland Place (the modern 49), on the northwest corner of Weymouth Street. In 1822, from the pavement outside the Embassy, or from its rearward upstairs windows, he looked straight down Weymouth Street at his old lodgings, a quarter of a mile away—so these were indeed, as he says, "opposite" the Embassy. The same view is visible to this day, for Portland Place and Weymouth Street remain little altered.[11]

I could sense a timeline emerging. If Mary Neale had been responsible for helping Chateaubriand find this garret on Paradise Street in 1793, and if she had been twelve years old at the time, she would have been seventeen when Chateaubriand described her as a beautiful woman at what would have been a second meeting with her in 1798 at Mrs. O'Leary's home, and she would have been eighteen in 1799, when she married Patrick Fallon. This scenario showed how known facts could fit my family's recollections, but could it be verified?

When I unexpectedly had an opportunity to visit London with relatives, I seized it, realizing that at last I could become personally acquainted with the streets walked by the young François-René and Mary Neale. After arriving in London, I booked a hotel room near Moxon Street, the "Paradise Street" of Chateaubriand's day. Around the corner from the hotel was Paddington Gardens, a contemporary park fashioned from the graveyard that had haunted the recuperating Chateaubriand in fall 1793. Children playing in that park today surely have no idea that beneath them are resting the remains of innumerable souls from centuries ago. Nor are they likely aware that Moxon

Street was once called "Paradise Street" because it led directly to a cemetery and thus to paradise. It is possible to still see the old designation of Paradise Street in faded paint on the brick wall of one of the buildings. Further, on a wrought-iron fence protecting the park there is a handsome brass plaque, installed in 1981 by the Société Chateaubriand and the French ambassador after Dr. Painter's analysis and independent research by two French scholars had determined that Chateaubriand had lived in an attic garret somewhere in the neighborhood, although the exact location was unknown. The plaque contains the following inscription:

> The author of *Mémoires d'outre-tombe*
> Chateaubriand
> lived as an émigré in a garret near to this
> site and began his literary career.
> He returned in 1822 as French ambassador
> and resided in Portland Place.

Later I went to St. George's Church of Hanover Square. It looks today much as it did in 1799, when Patrick and Mary were married there. Its architecture, by the noted student of Christopher Wren, John James, was much admired at its dedication in 1725, such that maintenance and renovations in the late nineteenth and twentieth centuries faithfully strove to retain its character. I asked the clerk in the office if she could suggest any means of obtaining further information about Patrick Fallon, who was shown on the marriage license as being "of St. Marylebone." She told me the Marylebone Library maintained genealogical records that might have information about Fallons then living in the district.

That evening I went to the library, but a search for the name Fallon produced nothing in all the indexes I consulted. As I was about to leave, I passed a small file-box labeled Deeds. I searched it for the name Fallon, without success; under the name Neale, however, I found a reference that read: "Neale, Th.; No. 460." When checking the Catalogue of Deeds under number 460, I discovered that it conveyed a deed of land in 1786 to "Thomas Neale, the elder, of Paradise Street, builder." Neale, of Paradise Street!

Realizing my likely proximity to information about young Mary Neale and the famous Frenchman, I felt my pulse accelerate and requested the deed, a large vellum document decorated with beautiful hand-inscribed calligraphy, from which I photographed signatures. One witness to the deed appeared to be Thomas Neale Jr., whose signature looked different from that of Thomas Neale, the elder, also listed. Also, I inferred, a descriptive phrase such as "the elder" would not have been necessary had there not also been a younger Thomas Neale, who was likely an apprentice to his father.

I turned next to the records of city taxes preserved on 35mm photographic reels. There I found an entry in 1786 for No. 8 Paradise Street, showing "Thomas Neale and Shop" with tax payments of 24 shillings for the residence and 8 for the shop. Then I sought the tax records for 1793, the year Chateaubriand resided on Paradise Street, and found an entry for "Thomas Neale, Esq.," this time at No. 10 Paradise Street. It stated, "James Curtis moves in at Christmas," implying that Thomas Neale vacated the premises in December 1793. I knew from other sources that Chateaubriand left London for Beccles that very month.

At closing time, I had to leave the library. Overnight I was perplexed about the change in address and the apparent departure of Mr. Neale. Perhaps he died, but aside from Chateaubriand, what became of the other occupants of that multistory house? Intent on assembling more pieces of the puzzle, I returned to the library early the next morning and researched Mr. Neale's tax records for

each year from 1786 through 1793, coming upon the following
information:

Year	Occupant	Address	Tax
1786	Thomas Neale & Shop	No. 8	24 shillings 8 shillings
1787	Thomas Neale & Shop	No. 8	24 8
1788	Thomas Neale & Shop	No. 12	24 8
1789	Thomas Neale & Shop	No. 12	24 8
1790	Thomas Neale & Shop	No. 10	24 8
1791	Thomas Neale, Esq.	No. 10	32
1792	Thomas Neale, Esq.	No. 10	32
1793	Thomas Neale, Esq.	No. 10	32 (James Curtis moves in at Christmas)

At first, it seemed odd to me that Thomas Neale would be
relocating so frequently, from No. 8 to No. 12 to No. 10 Paradise
Street, especially given the large shop he needed for his trade as
a builder. Then I noticed that his neighbors on either side also
seemed to be moving, simultaneously and symmetrically; and I
realized that no one had moved but rather city authorities had
created a new numbering scheme for the street. Neither was there
reason to assume that Thomas Neale, the elder, had disappeared
or died; most likely he occupied the multistory flat continuously

from 1786 through 1793, though perhaps his son and other relatives lived with him. I then located a Horwood's map published in January 1794, showing that No. 10 Paradise Street was one house away from the "burying ground" (see figure 8), a perfect location for its skylight to have provided a view of the graveyard below, as Chateaubriand had described his dwelling.

The documents I found could not prove conclusively that a girl named Mary Neale lived on Paradise Street with relatives, perhaps a father, grandfather, or uncle named Thomas. Mr. Lowe succeeded in finding a will for Thomas Neale, the elder, prepared four years prior to his death in 1816 at age eighty, showing that he left most of his wealth and possessions to his son, Thomas Neale, Jr. There was no mention of Mary Neale Fallon, although granddaughters with other names were listed. Nonetheless, when I pieced Mr. Painter's findings together what I knew from my family story, the only conclusion I could reasonably draw was that the girl Mary Neale was there. The documents pointed to the exact location of Chateaubriand's attic garret of 1793 and placed the girl in the same house.

My next stop was Kensington Gardens, a comfortable walk from Paradise Street. In his memoirs, Chateaubriand described how, as a twenty-five-year-old in terrible distress in late summer 1793, he would head to Kensington Gardens, sit under a pine tree, and draft the essays and stories he hoped to publish, including the novella *René*:

I would make my way in those days towards Kensington or Westminster. Kensington pleased me; I would walk in the secluded part, while the part adjacent to Hyde Park was filled by a brilliant multitude. The contrast between my poverty and their wealth, my isolation and the crowd, suited me...[12]

Unsure whether pines were growing in Kensington Gardens at that time, I wrote to the Royal Parks Management. The response of the arboricultural manager, Ian Rodger, pointed out that in a plan from 1784 a small corner of the park had been designated the "fir quarter" and planted with Scots pines. This spot, just below Oxford Road (today's Bayswater Road) near the Inverness Gate, thus certainly contained pines dating back to Chateaubriand's time in the area, and afforded a view of Hyde Park across today's artificial lake called the "long water." Rodger concluded, "Limited evidence admittedly, but I think M. Chateaubriand could very well have been sitting at the foot of a pine tree!"

Chateaubriand's reverie continued:

> I would gaze at the young English girls passing by in the distance with the same confusion of desire that I had in former times felt for my Sylphide, after I had dressed her to suit my follies and hardly dared to raise my eyes to my work. Death, which I believed was fast approaching, added mystery to this vision of the world I was about to abandon. Did anyone pause to gaze at the stranger sitting at the foot of the pine tree? Did some pretty woman sense René's invisible presence?[13]

In one of Painter's letters to me, dated January 5, 1993, he wondered whether Mary "could have been one of the girls Chateaubriand saw passing in Kensington Gardens that summer, while he sat under a pine tree writing. . . . It would be just like him to make such a vague anonymous allusion to a meeting that actually happened and had further consequences." The facts lined up neatly. My family's oral history maintained that Mary was a schoolgirl who passed time in a park near her school and paused when she saw a gentleman and took pity on him. This is consistent with Mary being one of the "English girls" passing by, pausing "to gaze at the stranger," and being "some pretty woman" who not only sensed René's invisible presence but befriended Chateaubriand and brought him to lodge at the house where she lived.

At this point, I began reflecting on Mary's age. With no birth record for her, I could only speculate. According to the oral history handed down to me, she was twelve years old in the park, a detail that could have changed in successive retellings. There was also the fact that a woman was supposed to have attained twenty-one years of age to qualify for a marriage license. Although Mary could have been younger and falsely asserted that she was twenty-one when applying for her marriage license in 1799, in the absence of evidence to the contrary it seemed reasonable to assume that she may have indeed been twenty-one at the time. If this were true, then she would have been about fifteen when, as "some pretty woman," she met Chateaubriand in Kensington Gardens and twenty when, as a "tall beautiful young Irish woman," he observed her at the home of Mrs. O'Leary.

Hoping her school records would help me establish her age while having lunch at the park, I considered the most likely possibilities. As a builder, Thomas Neale, the elder, was certainly wealthy enough to have provided Mary with a good education, perhaps at a school on Oxford Road, which bordered Kensington Gardens at the then fir quarter. In those days, fine schools for young women were plentiful in that area though generally short-lived, often opening under the auspices of a well-educated headmistress and closing when she left. Thus, there are records of advertisements for such schools but no surviving school records. However, it is entirely possible that as a schoolgirl on Oxford Road between the ages of twelve and fifteen, Mary Neale could have gone with her classmates to the park, taken snacks there, met the desperate Frenchman, and invited him to lodge at her house.

Reminiscing about 1798, a time when he resided in the home of Mrs. O'Leary, Chateaubriand described Mary Neale as having blossomed into a tall beautiful young Irish woman under the escort of a *tuteur*, a French word with multiple meanings in English. A nineteenth-century English rendering translates the word as "guardian,"[14] which is proper even today, while a twenty-first-century translation, "tutor,"[15] is also correct but seems out of place in this context. I believe Chateaubriand is stressing only that the tea party was an occasion for which it would have been appropriate, given the etiquette of the day, for a single woman to have a trustworthy escort. Being a man of short stature, Chateaubriand's use of the adjective *tall* perhaps suggested itself because she may have been taller than he was. One year later, as documents prove, Mary lived not in St. Marylebone Parish but in St. George Parish, and married Patrick Fallon, naming her first-born son Thomas, the given name of the male elders in her family.

As for Chateaubriand, he surely began his literary career in 1793 as summer faded into fall and winter. Believing that he was close to death, he likely considered the lodgings on Paradise Street, bare as they were, a secure home where he might recover. Indeed, it was there that his reviving energy soon unleashed his imagination to create the works he knew would ensure his fame. He must have attributed his subsequent renown and fortune, if not his life, to the intervention of the Irish girl. Years later he could have been a concerned companion offering advice when, as a young adult, she struggled to make decisions about her own future.

My research thus far had revealed that the girl in my family story, Mary O'Neill, was actually Mary Eliza Neale, a middle-class woman who was likely the beneficiary of a cultivated education and who found security in marrying Patrick Fallon, a merchant with a comfortable income. Beyond those details, there was ample evidence that Chateaubriand provided Mary or members of her family with money during her adult life and that he assured an outstanding French Catholic education for her eldest son, Thomas. What could have been his motivation?

If Chateaubriand believed he was the father of Thomas, there was legal reason for him to have hidden his interest in the boy. In the late eighteenth and early nineteenth centuries, it was common for paternity searches to dislocate or even destroy otherwise stable families. As a result, a provision of French revolutionary law, consolidated in the Napoleonic Code of 1804, was a ban on paternity searches and on third-party child support. In short, not only scandal but serious judicial consequences would ensue should Chateaubriand have sought to claim paternity of Thomas.

Many details of Mary's life remained elusive. Without baptismal records, I could only guess at her age when described as a schoolgirl at the park in 1793. Based on family oral history, she was twelve, but she could have been older. Further, I did not know her relationship with the other members of the Neale family at 10 Paradise Street; my family story consistently referred to the two elders in her home as her aunt and uncle, never her parents. Nor did I find a record of an inheritance directed to her from anyone.

I did now know that the Neale family moved out of its longtime home on Paradise Street in the dead of winter. I knew, too, that when Mary married Patrick she was in a different part of town, St. George Parish, but I had no address for her. Nor did I know whether she was still in the company of members of the Neale family, though her elegant confident signature led me to imagine she was happy at her wedding. My challenge at this point was to learn everything I could about her first child, Thomas— my great-great-grandfather.

CHAPTER 4

Tracing the Trajectory
of Thomas

LIFE BECKONS.

Mary's son Thomas came of age in the first two decades of the nineteenth century, a propitious time to discover the world. The two most consequential political revolutions in the recent history of Western civilization, American and French, had occurred, setting much of society in a new direction. Industrialization, with its promise of automation, comfort, and convenience, was in its earliest stages. Art was flourishing with the powerful literary genre of the novel, intoxicating new poetry attracting the description "romantic," new forms of music in the radical compositions of Beethoven, and florid paintings of portraits and dramatic tableaux. Ordinary citizens could sense new possibilities for the fulfillment of life goals unimaginable one or two generations earlier. A young man with a superior education could harbor high expectations.

Discovery of the marriage license had revealed that Thomas's father, Patrick, was a merchant with known financial standing, enough to post a large bond. Indeed, it seems certain that Thomas was born into a secure family household. In registers for the 1790s, there is a listing for Peter Fallon, hatter, at 9 Edwards Street, in the St. Marylebone Parish, not far from Paradise Street. Peter was likely the father of Patrick Fallon, and in the 1805 edition of *Holden's Triennial Directory* there is a listing for Patrick Fallon, hatter, at 27 Mortimer Street, even closer to Paradise Street. By 1812, the shop was located in a more upscale commercial area, at 85 Piccadilly; a year later it was situated in an affluent shopping area, at 23 Suffolk Street, near Charing Cross, and named Fallon & Co., Hat Manufactory. In the 1813 issue of *Gentlemen's Quarterly*, there is a notice for Fallon, Fanche & Co., hatmakers to the royal family. Although this may only mean that the company's headwear was sold to someone with a royal title, it suggests the shop had high respectability. Finally, the shop was moved to the City of London, the busiest commercial district, where it was listed continuously until at least 1836 as Fallon, Fanche & Co., 8 King William Street. These increasingly prominent business locations indicate that Patrick Fallon was a successful tradesman and merchant.

As members of a growing middle class in early nineteenth-century London, the Patrick Fallon family could have afforded good educations for their children. But what was not yet possible in England at that time was a superior Catholic education, which, according to my family story, Chateaubriand had offered to Thomas. Catholic schooling had been eliminated in England after the ascension of Elizabeth I to the English throne in 1558. The Protestant Reformation had consolidated the Anglican Church, bolstered by anti-Catholic sentiment and legislation. Therefore, in 1593 the College of St. Omer was established on the European continent so that English boys whose families remained Catholic could benefit from teaching sanctioned by the Church. St. Omer remained for centuries a beacon for elite English Catholic families, educating, among others, an English aristocrat named Thomas Weld in the mid-eighteenth century.

After England's easing of legal restrictions against Catholic practices in 1791, Catholic schools had gradually appeared there once more. The most famous, the Jesuit College of Stonyhurst, was in fact the former College of St. Omer moved to an estate in rural Lancashire by its student Thomas Weld. In 1794, Weld had deeded a run-down mansion and associated buildings, along with thirty acres of land, to the Jesuits, who then reestablished in that location the school that had been exiled to the European continent for the previous two centuries. As Thomas Fallon came of age in the early nineteenth century, Stonyhurst was gradually becoming a secure source for advanced Catholic education, but its quality was perceived as nowhere near that of the royal academies in Catholic France that had been reestablished following the defeat of Napoleon. Consequently, for Mary and Patrick Fallon, Chateaubriand's offer was a rare opportunity to enhance the life prospects of their eldest child.

With the information I had gathered, I finally felt ready to write to the leading Chateaubriand scholar, Pierre Riberette, editor in chief of the massive *Correspondance Générale,* a complete critical edition of Chateaubriand's known letters and materials. By this time, I knew that my research, having produced knowledge of profound importance to Chateaubriand scholarship, needed to be shared with him. It also seemed to me that he might possess knowledge important to my quest. A few weeks later, I received a grateful letter from the amazed Professor Riberette. Rendered in carefully drawn French script using black fountain pen ink, it was dated April 2, 1993, and covered four pages, front and back, opening with the formal salutation "Cher Monsieur":

> Your letter came as a great surprise to me, but also brought me great satisfaction, and I should like to express my sincerest thanks to you....You see, for the last 60 years, Chateaubriand specialists have actively concerned themselves with "the Fallon affair."

> Indeed, Maurice Levaillant discusses the young Mr. Fallon: "Young Fallon seems to have spent only a year in Amiens. The honors board does not mention his name. It would be nice to know what the precise link is between Chateaubriand and that schoolboy who was 16–17 years old in 1817, exactly 17 years after Chateaubriand came back from England....Did his famous protector carry on taking an interest in him? What became of him?"[1]

I suppose that Dame Joan Evans got all her information from Levaillant's book and that she is the one who drew the obvious conclusion: that Fallon was Chateaubriand's son, but the date of Patrick Fallon's marriage with Mary Neale makes this link highly unlikely—which fact will disappoint many of Chateaubriand's admirers, who would have preferred him to have had a child.

Levaillant knew that Chateaubriand had declared bankruptcy in 1817, unable even to keep his home. So Levaillant was startled, as any Chateaubriand scholar would be, to learn that Chateaubriand was paying tuition and fees for an unknown boy at an excellent school, apparently the only nonhousehold expense he chose to bear that year. Since Levaillant's discovery of Chateaubriand's letters to his financial agent, Le Moine, occurred around 1920, long before the destruction of school records during the German invasion of 1940, Levaillant was able to find a file at the school showing registration for the year 1817 of "Fallon, Thomas—né à Londres." He thus conjectured that Thomas was a student at Amiens for only one year and was sixteen or seventeen in 1817.

Several items of evidence passed down in my family, however, offered alternative perspectives. One was a document that had survived over generations and ended up in my father's files, which led me to believe, in contrast to Levaillant, that Thomas had remained at Amiens for a four-year term. It was a type of visa ensuring Thomas safe passage from Paris to Boulogne sur Mer, a customary port for ships going from France to England. The document was signed in Paris by the English ambassador, Charles Stuart, and dated July 16, 1821; it was unusual for the ambassador himself to issue an ordinary visa, but Charles Stuart was a colleague of Chateaubriand's. The document bore a French government stamp and acknowledgment marked "Boulogne, July 17, 1821." Since the time span between 1817 and 1821 is four years, the normal period for obtaining a degree from a French collège royal, it seems plausible that Thomas studied at Amiens for four years and then returned home to England in summer 1821. Therefore, it is likely that after completing his studies at Amiens, he traveled to Paris, where Chateaubriand helped him secure the travel documents he needed to return to England. Thomas could have been sixteen or seventeen years old when he arrived at Amiens in 1817, although in those days younger boys, beginning at about age fourteen, also matriculated at a typical French collège royal like the one at Amiens.

To better assess Thomas's age, I turned to another gift from my father. Referred to with ritual gravity as Papá Tomás, it was an oil portrait of Thomas (see figure 9) that had hung in a dark corner of our house all my life. I had not looked at it closely until Thomas emerged as central to solving the puzzle that launched me on my quest. I took the painting to a master craftsman, who cleaned and restored it. Then I sent photographs of it to the curator of early nineteenth-century works at the National Portrait Gallery in London, Dr. Peter Funnell. I thought the painting might have been commissioned by Chateaubriand during his ambassadorship to London and given to the young man. Chateaubriand arrived as ambassador in April 1822, only ten months after Thomas had left France, although neither one could have imagined such a circumstance in summer 1821. Chateaubriand very likely would have looked up the young man whose education he had assured, and procured for him a gift, such as a portrait of the kind that was popular at that time.

Funnell replied in a letter dated August 31, 1993:

The costume, and hairstyle, would date it to the years around 1820.…The style of the portrait has a looseness which I would associate more with English painting at this time, but which certainly should not make us rule out a French artist.…As far as we could tell from photographs, the support for the picture would appear to be some sort of panel or board, possibly millboard. Millboards of this size are quite common as supports in English painting at this time which might reinforce the feeling that it was English. To my eye, the portrait is a work of some quality, done by a professional hand and not a commonplace product of an everyday craftsman.… It is not a formal or public portrait: the fact that it stayed in your ancestor's possession confirms that it was done for private purposes, perhaps as a token of friendship.

Funnell's general assessment, and my subsequent verification that the painting's support was indeed millboard, strengthened my belief that the work had been completed in 1822, during Chateaubriand's sojourn in the English capital at the height of his fame and career. If Thomas had been born around 1800, which would have been necessary for Chateaubriand to have been his father, then the young man in the portrait would have been about twenty-two years old. Some scholars I have consulted are struck immediately by the resemblance between the young man in the portrait and the existing likenesses of Chateaubriand, especially the jutting chin, the large ears, the sloping shoulders, the curly black hair, and the fair complexion. A few French admirers of Chateaubriand have found the portrait convincing enough to consider Thomas his son. Nonetheless, all the evidence I had examined thus far could not silence stubborn questions that plagued me, much less settle the burning question of whether Chateaubriand's uncommon interest in Thomas was paternal. Were my father and I, as well as our forebears, biological descendants of the charismatic Frenchman?

My quest for details about my great-great-grandfather's life continued with a trip to Colombia. Every five years or so I was in the habit of returning to Bogotá to maintain contact with my relatives. I had been keeping my cousins informed of my efforts to clarify the family story about Chateaubriand and Mary. When I let them know I would soon be returning, they began to look through their effects for clues to missing parts of our family story. Surprisingly, my relatives discovered two key items that provided significant new information. One item was a large oil portrait of a mature Thomas, perhaps in his late forties, painted in Colombia around 1845, found hanging in the home of my cousin Marcela Samper de Angel, one of his descendants. Although the face in the portrait reveals a more developed personality than in the earlier portrait, the features shared with the physiognomy of Chateaubriand at a comparable age seem just as striking (see figure 10).

The other item unearthed by my relatives—a French passport issued to Thomas in the name of the king, found stored under the bed of my cousin Pablo Quijano-Samper—proved to be a revelation. It had been issued in Amiens on December 19, 1818, for a trip from there to London, probably so that Thomas could spend the Christmas season with his parents. It described Thomas as a pupil at the Collège Royal of Amiens. Issued long before the invention of photographs, the passport teems with information allowing an examiner to determine the identity of the person presenting it. It revealed multiple physical details, for example, describing Thomas's hair and eyebrows as light brown, his forehead as low, his eyes as blue, his nose as ordinary, his mouth as average, his chin as round, his expression as plain, and his complexion as florid. It also displays his elegant and confident signature. It seems erroneous, though, in recording his height as a mere 1.40 meters (four feet seven inches). Thomas could hardly have been this short at age eighteen. The early 1800s were a time of transition in units of measurement, however, with the metric system only recently adopted and a variety of older measuring methods still in occasional use. Despite these minute details about Thomas, unfortunately the passport lacks the one fact I sought most avidly: a date of birth. It comes close, nonetheless, clearly stating his age as eighteen and his status as a native of London (see figures 11.1 and 11.2).

Consequently, although Thomas's date of birth was still in question, the hypothesis that he had been only fourteen in 1817 had to be abandoned. Levaillant was clearly right to assume that Thomas was about seventeen upon arriving in Amiens, but he was apparently wrong to guess that Thomas remained at the school only for a single year, from mid-1817 to mid-1818. The passport proves that Thomas was at the school during the following year, at least until December 1818, and probably continuing for the rest of that school year.

Still hoping to find a record of birth for Thomas, I remembered that decades earlier I had spent time with my father's mother, Doña Blanca Convers de Fallon, taking notes about the family history. She was then ninety-two years old and still in command of a memory as sharply disciplined as in her youth. I searched for the notes and saw that she had told me Thomas had had two brothers, Cornelius and Daniel, and that there might have been one more brother, named James. Armed with this news, I wrote once more to the genealogist in London, Mr. Lowe, asking him to again look for birth records.

It seemed to me that since the Fallons were devout Catholics they had probably sought the services of Catholic priests surreptitiously, perhaps via the embassies of nations whose state religion was Catholicism. Concentrating the search on those locations, Mr. Lowe discovered records for both of Thomas's brothers in the baptismal registry of the chapel of the Portuguese Embassy in London. A chapel register contained the inscription "Cornelius Edwin, son of Patrick Fallon and Mary Eliza Neale, his wife" with a birth date of April 5, 1809. The entry "Daniel Cajetan, son of Patrick Fallon and Mary Eliza, his wife" was recorded later, showing a birth date of August 6, 1812. Thomas Fallon, who would then have been about twelve years old, was listed as Daniel Cajetan's godfather, and his signature adorned the record along with the signatures of Mary and Patrick. Despite exhaustive efforts, however, we never succeeded in finding a birth record for Thomas, or for a brother named James. The large gap in years between the birth dates of the three brothers suggested the possibility of intervening miscarriages or even the death of a child, which could have been the missing James.

Further investigation revealed that by 1836 ownership of the hat shop had been transferred to Thomas's next eldest brother, Cornelius, who was married that year. The wedding register named

Patrick Fallon as a witness, but there was no mention of Mary Eliza. Cornelius's first wife died, and he remarried in 1841. Again Patrick Fallon was mentioned in the wedding register, but not Mary. In addition, a civil record was located reporting Patrick's death in 1846 at age seventy-nine, indicating that he would have been about thirty-two when he married Mary Eliza in 1799, practically the same age as Chateaubriand. It also showed that at the time of his death Patrick was living with a woman named Sarah Foley.

Another avenue of investigation became apparent when, while walking to work one morning, I recalled that as an undergraduate student I had spent a semester at the University of Tübingen, Germany, and, being a foreigner, had been required to register with the police to obtain a residence permit. It dawned on me that Thomas, as a foreigner in Amiens, had probably also been required to register with the police. I decided to write once more to the archivist at Amiens and ask for a search of police records that might have survived the 1940 German assault. I enclosed a copy of the passport I had recently discovered, realizing it had probably been issued by the Amiens police.

A few weeks later I received a reply from Isabel Neuschwander, director of archives for the Département de la Somme, the county whose capital city is Amiens. She replied that she had been unable to find Thomas's birth date but could report another astonishing discovery. In the basement of the police department were bins of old files, including one, marked "#T_85," containing notes of financial affairs associated with the Collège Royal. In that bin, she and her colleagues had discovered, bound together by a yellow ribbon attached to a tag labeled "the young Fallon," a packet of three documents, photocopies of which she was delighted to include.

The key document was a handwritten letter dated May 29, 1818, from the minister of the interior, Count Joseph Lainé, a member of the king's cabinet. In the margins of this letter were notes written by Count Alexandre Louis d'Allonville, prefect of the Département de la Somme, the king's royal appointee responsible for administration of Amiens and its county. The minister of the interior's letter to the prefect read as follows:

Dear Mr. Count: You brought to my attention in your letter of the 9th of this month the situation of the young Fallon, English by birth, boarding student at the Collège Royal of Amiens where he was supported to this day by <u>M. le Vicomte de Chateaubriand</u> and who is at the point of being abandoned by his protector. Considering the reasons given in your letter I thought it my duty to propose to the King the appointment of this child to a government scholarship. I enclose the letter of notice of this appointment and I am writing to the Principal to let him know His Majesty's decision.

> With kindest regards, Mr. Count,
> Yours Sincerely,
> The Minister Secretary of State of the Interior
> Lainé

In the margins of the letter, the prefect Count d'Allonville had written the following five notations:

1. Response to my letter sent on May 9, 1818 (Nr. 364 Cabinet).
2. Announce to the young Fallon his appointment as royal pupil, without any other details, other than that the minister proposed him to the King upon a report of the prefect.

3. Send to the principal a summary of the enclosed appointment.

4. The young Fallon, english [*sic*], boarder at the Collège Royal of Amiens, appointed Royal Pupil with full scholarship starting June 1, 1818.

5. Letter of May 29, 1818, to the young Fallon confirming his appointment. Letter of the same day to the principal of the Collège Royal, asking him to deliver the letter to the young Fallon. (See figure 12.)

The two other documents contained in the packet were a copy of the letter of appointment informing Thomas of his royal scholarship and a copy of the requirements necessary to complete registration at the college as a royal pupil. All three documents showed that the prefect's May 9 letter to the minister of the interior had resulted in Thomas successfully receiving a scholarship.

Other sources confirm that in 1818 Chateaubriand was at the end of his rope, having declared bankruptcy and forfeited property to pay debts he had accrued. He had sold his most treasured possessions, including his library and, most painfully, his beloved estate in the Valley of the Wolves outside Paris. He received a small income associated with his title of viscount, but otherwise very little revenue. The costs of supporting Thomas—including his tuition, books, and living expenses, for the year 1817–1818—had been paid, but subsequent financing was beyond Chateaubriand's ability. He must have written of his distress to the principal of the college, and the principal must have written to the prefect. It is doubtful that the principal would have acted if Thomas had not been a superior student.

Unfortunately, I do not have a copy of the prefect's letter dated May 9 to the minister of the interior. All letters in those days were written by hand, occasionally summarized for a file, but rarely copied. Clearly the prefect's letter had been persuasive, given the interior minister's acknowledgment of the reasons for the crisis. That the issuance of the scholarship funds hinged on the status of Chateaubriand is evident from the fact that in the minister's letter only the name of Viscount Chateaubriand is conspicuously underlined.

Although Chateaubriand had been sacked, humiliated by the court eighteen months earlier, he was still a renowned public figure and a potential candidate for the king's service sometime in the future. Those learning about the boy in May 1818, including the prefect, the interior minister, and the king, must have wondered about Chateaubriand's dedicated efforts to support him. They may well have drawn the same inference as Chateaubriand scholars more than a hundred years later that the Frenchman's concerns were paternal, if illicit. The interior minister did not delay in making a recommendation to the king, who then provided an expeditious approval.

Once the matter had been decided, the prefect made a point of telling his orderly to inform Thomas of this extraordinary honor but not divulge details of how it came about. We can guess that Thomas was surprised and assumed it had something to do with his performance at school. Similarly, Chateaubriand may not have known that the king's personal hand was responsible for his providential rescue from a financial responsibility that had become impossible to sustain. As for Mary and Patrick, they must have been proud of their son, unaware that Chateaubriand had been on the verge of discontinuing his support of Thomas's schooling.

Excited by the materials received from the archivist in Amiens, I made plans to visit the city and photograph the original documents. The authorities in Amiens surprised me by booking me into a hotel room with a window overlooking the school, where I could watch the students at play during their periods of recess. As their voices in excitable school-age French drifted up toward my window, I imagined I was listening to the voices of boys and young men of almost two centuries ago, among them the shouts of my great-great-grandfather. Later I walked the halls and ascended the stone staircases that my ancestor had climbed during his four years of matriculation, imagining the footsteps, the rustling of school materials, and the muffled conversations of pupils and teachers from long ago echoing through the stone corridors.

The thrill I felt being in this place was augmented by the excitement of the archivist and other colleagues involved in the search. They regaled me with stories about how the packet had appeared when they opened the bin in which it had been stored almost two hundred years earlier.

I wrote to Professor Riberette with the news, which he found electrifying. His enthusiasm carried him quickly to the Royal Archives in Paris to see if he could confirm the events from the king's files. Although he could not find the prefect's letter of May 9 or a birth date for Thomas, he was able to verify the following facts: King Louis XVIII provided scholarships to dozens of aspiring students; the funds for these scholarships came from the king's private bursary and not the state treasury; the scholarship for Thomas was the only one for which no first name was provided—simply "the young Fallon"—and no reason for the award was given; and Thomas was the only recipient not classified as a French national. The grant to Thomas was exceptional, like no other.

Subsequently, Thomas received full support, which meant that, in addition to tuition, he was provided with room and board and an allowance for books, supplies, and personal expenses. The curriculum involved instruction in Greek and Latin, classical and modern literature, art, music, mathematics, and the developing fields of biology, chemistry, and physics. A graduate of the Collège Royal could be assured of competence sufficient to pursue a variety of occupations, including branches of medicine, business, and what we today call engineering. By the time of his graduation at age twenty-one, Thomas had acquired more intellectual capital than most anyone else his age. He was ready to launch an independent life and career.

My quest had by now not only revealed significant tangible evidence of my ancestors' relationship to Chateaubriand but also stirred up many questions. It was time to assemble as much of the puzzle as I could, perhaps adding new pieces to complete the picture, thus reaching a solution.

CHAPTER 5

Arriving at
a Finish Line

CONUNDRUMS CLARIFY.

If my father had passed me a baton in a marathon moving from one generation to the next, I was determined to be the last to hold it, to carry it across the finish line. My scholarly instincts flashed caution. Even though I had assembled more facts than I had imagined possible and had exercised sound logic in drawing conclusions about them, I knew there would likely be lingering ambiguity. Even so, I could not ignore the obligation I felt to make sense of what the past was telling me.

To my surprise, a focused search of the past had yielded treasures, showing that an earnest quest can indeed transport us into lives from a time long gone. The work is never fully done, however, because fresh lines of inquiry inevitably arise, hovering as tantalizing fruit. I was sure that telling records buried under the weight of time and history could eventually still be found. I was less certain, though, that any future discoveries would disrupt the trajectory of the story that was already taking shape, emerging from the dust cloud of a past lived consequentially by those who dared, loved, and suffered in the same ways as people of every other time and place.

Therefore the task, it seemed, was to add informed imagination to investigation and thereby coherently flesh out, with as much accuracy as possible, the story told by my ancestors. What had been revealed as fact had to serve as an anchoring framework for an account in which true human motives and feelings would forever be partially obscured. Interpretation remains the craft of history. Because any story is only one of several that could arise from the same known facts, the following story—the one that seems to best fit the facts—can only persuade by its ability to tie the evidence together plausibly.

It begins with Mary, the Irish girl who inspired the family tale and then vanished into mystery. The oral history of my family maintained that she lived in London with an aunt and uncle in a house with an attic garret that sheltered Chateaubriand when he was most vulnerable. A deed proves that the house was owned by Thomas Neale, the elder. He had a son named Thomas Neale, who might have lived there too. It is not known how either of them may have been related to Mary, perhaps as father or uncle, or who paid for Mary's superior education. Thomas Neale, the elder, died at the age of eighty in early July 1816. He wrote his will in 1807 and added a codicil in 1812. The lengthy will makes provisions for four granddaughters and a sister, none named Neale or Fallon, and yields the bulk of his estate to his son Thomas. At the time of his death, Thomas Neale, the elder, was living in St. Marylebone Parish at Charlotte Row, about ten blocks northwest of 10 Paradise Street, the home where he, Mary, and Chateaubriand lived in fall 1793. In March 1799, Mary's marriage listing in the register of St. George's Church of Hanover Square showed her residence in St. George Parish, at least ten blocks southeast of 10 Paradise Street, her exact address unknown.

Chateaubriand wrote that he encountered a tall, beautiful young Irish woman, Mary Neale, at a tea party in spring 1798, escorted by a guardian. If, as my family's oral history suggests, Mary was twelve years old when she first met Chateaubriand in 1793, then she would have been seventeen when she encountered him again in 1798 and eighteen at her wedding. If instead she were at least twenty-one at her wedding, as required for a marriage license, she could have been fifteen or more in 1793, but likely not younger than twelve. She would have then been about twenty when meeting Chateaubriand again and twenty-one at her wedding. It is not known with whom was she living in 1798 or the identity of the guardian. Perhaps she was in the care of the younger Thomas Neale, whose will I have not found and about whom I know very little. As a well-educated adult, Mary made a good marriage to an established merchant, Patrick Fallon, and named her firstborn child Thomas, a name traditional to the Neale family. Although I do not have an exact date of birth for Thomas Fallon, I have indirect evidence from a French passport issued in 1818 that he was eighteen years old in December 1818, implying that he was born sometime in 1800.

Additionally, there is a shocking revelation about Mary's later life contained in a letter cited in Maurice Levaillant's 1922 publication of hitherto unknown letters from Chateaubriand to his financial agent in Paris, M. Le Moine. Chateaubriand's letter, written in Lausanne, Switzerland, on June 7, 1826, includes the instruction: "To you will appear again a poor English woman named Fallon. Give her 100 francs please…"[1]

This presents another conundrum since there is no mention of Mary's adulthood in the story related by my ancestors. What was Mary, impoverished, doing in Paris less than four years after Chateaubriand's brief sojourn in London as French ambassador? Mary's youngest son, Daniel Cajetan Fallon, was born August 6, 1812, making him thirteen years old in June 1826. Mary was a kind and attentive mother, or I would not have an oft-repeated family story that treats her with tender affection; I can't imagine that she would have willingly abandoned a child on the verge of adolescence. The next family record I have is of the marriage of Mary's second eldest son, Cornelius Edwin Fallon, on January 16, 1836, at which Patrick Fallon was a witness but Mary's presence was not documented. Therefore, it seems that Mary died, probably in Paris, sometime in 1826 or shortly thereafter. My inability to find a death record for Mary Eliza Neale Fallon in Paris may be because it was among the many civil records destroyed in the Paris uprisings of 1828, 1848, and 1870. Neither did I find a death record for her in London.

Discrepancies between Chateaubriand's documented behavior and his accounts about it in his memoirs could, it seems, offer clues about events he sought to obscure or hide, thus revealing some details about his relationship with Mary. One such discrepancy concerns why Chateaubriand abruptly left London in December 1793. He asserts in his memoirs that he left London for Beccles in December 1793 to assist an antiquarian society in writing a history of the county of Suffolk because he could interpret French documents from the eleventh century. Assiduous scholarship has subsequently proven, however, that no such society existed and no such history was undertaken. Pierre Riberette describes Chateaubriand's claim in the following way:

> Having been recommended by another compatriot émigré, the journalist Peltier, he found work (although, rather

precarious it must be admitted) as a professor of French and perhaps also as a dancing master. He was attached to a school in the small town of Beccles, in Suffolk, and also gave private lessons to the neighboring young people. However, it is unimaginable that he would reveal this occupation, certainly mercenary but entirely honorable, in the *Mémoires d'outre-tombe*. Certainly not! Bearing in mind the admonition of one of his relatives, the old Abbot of Chateaubriand de La Guerrande, who declared that the Chateaubriands had private tutors, but were the private tutors of no one, he preferred to say that he had been employed by a local learned society (which, of course, never existed) to research a collection of manuscripts (of which no one has ever heard, since they were the fruit of his own imagination).[2]

Indeed, from accounts by his contemporaries and Chateaubriand himself we know that at this time he found employment in Beccles as a teacher of French at a local school—a position he considered humiliating—and also gave French lessons to daughters of well-to-do families, as well as dancing lessons, an even greater abasement for a French aristocrat. Despite his avowal that he arrived in Beccles with secure and worthy employment in hand, his established behavior suggests he was floundering and made do with what he could find.

By applying imagination to the facts uncovered about the winter of 1793, it is possible to suspect that an unsettling cataclysm involving Mary and Chateaubriand led to his abrupt departure from London. Chateaubriand moved into the attic garret at 10 Paradise Street in October when, he reports, he was near death and desperate. Needing time to heal and attend to his ongoing writing projects, it is unlikely he would have contemplated moving out anytime soon. Then, too, would his landlord, Thomas Neale, the elder, have provided him with lodging knowing that the Neale family would be vacating the building in two months, as they did? And if Mr. Neale had had plans to move from a long-standing home containing his workshop would he have chosen to do so in the dead of a cold dark snowy London winter? Yet tax records show that a man named James Curtis moved in at Christmas, presumably taking ownership rather suddenly. Thereafter, no records have been found of the Neale family residing in the neighborhood. It seems plausible that some turn of events precipitated a hasty departure from 10 Paradise Street for everyone. It could have been alarm at a scandal involving the increasingly worrisome proximity of a twenty-five-year-old French émigré to a curious, intellectually sophisticated pubescent girl.

Chateaubriand describes his room in the attic garret as bleak and spare. His bed consisted of a mattress and a blanket. He mentions a chair, and there must have been a table with writing instruments, for he credits this lonely room as the spot where he unexpectedly found the breath of life returning and where he cemented his career as a writer. He entertained his colleague émigrés in this room and, for a time, shared the room with his cousin La Bouëtardais, who, gradually consumed by dementia, suffered a disabling stroke there. Most of the time Chateaubriand was alone, able to convert the fables of his rich imagination into ideas on paper, very likely putting finishing touches on the two novellas that later would ensure his success, *René* and *Atala*, as well as continuing to develop the essay on revolutions he had promised Peltier.

Mary, as an inquisitive schoolgirl responsible for his lodging, must have visited Chateaubriand in his attic room, probably bringing him meals from time to time and perhaps practicing her French with him. They likely would have spent time alone together, the solitude of each joining the other's. An acquaintance that ripens to friendship can advance through touch, smell, whisper, and fluttering heart to deeper intimacy. If Mary and Chateaubriand had been discovered together in a compromised circumstance, such a catastrophe could account for Chateaubriand's sudden departure to Beccles in the remote countryside, where he was obliged to seek a position as a teacher at a local school; such an event, and the Neale family's subsequent wish to avoid unseemly gossip could also explain their abrupt move from the neighborhood that had long been their home. Of course, other imagined explanations, ordinary and bland, might be applied to the same known facts. But we must account for Charlotte Ives.

Charlotte, the daughter of Reverend John Ives, married a distinguished naval officer, Samuel Sutton, twenty years her senior, in 1806. Admiral Sutton began his ten-year courtship of Charlotte, interrupted by absences at sea, about the same time that Chateaubriand was boarding in Charlotte's home at the invitation of her father.

Although Chateaubriand, in his memoirs, makes much of his declaration that he and Charlotte fell in love, his reminiscence is curiously devoid of ardor. He provides analytical descriptions about what life might have been like had he become a country gentleman by settling down in Bungay, and he comments that their ages were "in concord" for a young love, even though he was twenty-seven and she was fifteen in spring 1796. For the most part, he creates the impression that Charlotte's romantic interest in him was intensifying and he was flattered by it. The closest he came to showing affection is conveyed by a single sentence: "Little by little I felt the timid charm of attraction go forth from my soul."[3] He claimed that his dramatic flight from the situation was because he was already married. Yet Pierre Riberette has pointed out that his unwanted marriage to Céleste was a burden for him, and the Anglican Church would not have recognized a Catholic marriage anyway.[4] Consequently, if he had really wanted to stay and marry Charlotte he could have found a way.

After his abrupt departure from the Ives family home, Chateaubriand had no further contact with them for decades, leaving Charlotte in the lurch without explanation. Then, in early April 1822, a little more than a quarter century later, Chateaubriand returned triumphantly to England as French ambassador. In a characteristically evocative passage in his memoirs, he portrayed an episode of unexpected reconnection with Charlotte, which, he said, occurred shortly after his return to London:

One afternoon my footman came to tell me that a carriage had stopped outside the door, and that an English lady was asking to speak with me. As I have made it a rule, considering my public position, never to turn anyone away, I said the lady should be shown upstairs.

I was in my study when Lady Sutton was announced. I turned and saw a woman dressed in mourning, accompanied by two handsome boys also in mourning: one was about sixteen and the other about fourteen. I rose to meet the stranger and perceived that she was so overcome by emotion that she had difficulty walking. She said to me in a broken voice, "My Lord, do you recognize me?"

Yes, I recognized Miss Ives. The years that had passed over her head had left only their springtime behind. I took her hand, offered her a seat, and sat down beside her. I found myself unable to utter a word; my eyes welled up with tears, and through these tears I looked at her in silence. I felt, by the strength of what I was experiencing just how deeply I had loved her. Finally, I was able to say to her in turn, "And you, Madame, do you recognize me?"

She raised her eyes, which she had kept lowered, and appealed to me with a smiling and melancholy look that lingered like a long memory. Her hand was still between mine. Charlotte said to me: "I am in mourning for my mother. My father died several years ago. These young men are my children."

At these words, she withdrew her hand and fell back into the armchair, covering her face with her handkerchief.[5]

This passage illustrates Chateaubriand's masterful literary style but does little to bolster his veracity. The meeting he so movingly describes never took place in that way, as proven by documentary evidence.

In Chateaubriand's day, correspondence was frequent, since handwritten notes and letters were the only form of communication apart from a face-to-face meeting. Letters accumulated and were kept together for some time to refresh memory about details. Letters no longer of use were often discarded. When believed to harbor records of importance, they were saved in files. A good example is the trove of Chateaubriand letters discovered in the posthumous belongings of his financial agent, M. Le Moine. The custom of keeping letters is also apparent in nineteenth-century literature and stagecraft, which offer abundant examples of bundled letters kept as talismans of sentimentality or affairs of the heart. People wanting to shape their biographies for future generations often burned letters that, if preserved, might sully memories of the arc of life they sought to leave behind.

Chateaubriand was known to have burned large quantities of letters, especially after he left public service forever in 1830. Often, this painful task was undertaken with the assistance of his dearest friend, Madame Récamier, who occasionally saved some of the correspondence from the pyre. When she died, her property came to her niece, Madame Lenorment, who published several of the rescued letters in 1860. One short unpublished note, which may have been part of this treasure, could have passed through several unknown hands before coming to market at the Hotel Druout, an auction house in Paris, in the late twentieth century. It was ultimately purchased by the Chateaubriand Society and thus joined the archive curated by Pierre Riberette. Written in Chateaubriand's meticulous hand on a formal card rimmed with gold ink, it is dated May 14, 1822, and presents the following message:

> I have already, Madame, asked for news of you since arriving in England; I will never in all my life forget the people who gladly helped me in time of trouble. I will be honored to come visit you next Thursday at 2 o'clock, and to pay you my respects.

The note, signed by Chateaubriand, was folded inside an envelope addressed to Madame Sutton, whom he had earlier known as Charlotte Ives. It is similar to several he had sent to former acquaintances seeking to enjoy his company once more. Its formality is underscored by the sentence "I will never in all my life forget the people who gladly helped me in time of trouble," which appeared in precisely these words in notes he had sent to at least two other people, named Sophie Gay and Mr. Hamelin. In short, this message to Charlotte was obviously a pro forma acknowledgment of a letter from her, their first personal contact since their romance in Bungay. It proves that he was not at first visited by Charlotte Ives, as he writes in his memoirs, but that his initial encounter with her was in her lodging at her formal request and that he was fully aware of her identity.[6]

Charlotte's reported purpose in seeking a meeting with Chateaubriand that May, when she was temporarily in London, was to request assistance in obtaining a commission for her eldest son, who wished to go to India. Chateaubriand's colleague and friend George Canning had just been appointed governor-general of India, and Charlotte hoped that Chateaubriand could use his influence to secure her son's desired post. Indeed, Chateaubriand worked toward this goal, but before Canning could go to India he was promoted to the position of foreign secretary, so young Sutton remained in England.

Following Chateaubriand's May visit with Charlotte, according to his memoirs he met with her three more times in London. His characterizations of these meetings were embellished with beautifully crafted sentiments of love and affection. At the last of the meetings, he said, Charlotte gave him a packet of materials she had saved from their days in Bungay, telling him, "Don't be offended if I don't want to keep anything belonging to you." Chateaubriand took the packet back to his office and, in privacy, opened it with rising expectation. He observed disdainfully, however, that it contained only "a few trifling notes and a course of study with remarks on English and Italian poets."

In addition to the meetings between Chateaubriand and Charlotte in London, there was one more—in 1823 in Paris—after Chateaubriand had been appointed foreign minister by the king in December 1822 and was busy with affairs of state in pursuit of his multifaceted diplomatic career. Charlotte had brought her eldest son, Samuel, named after his father, to Paris to perfect his French, where she again sought a conversation with Chateaubriand about prospects for young Sutton. This meeting was short, formal, and ineffectual, leaving Charlotte hurt upon her return to England. Two letters from her ensued. In the first, which has not been preserved but which Chateaubriand described, she told him of her disappointment at his curt treatment of her in Paris and asked that he return the packet of materials she had given to him in London with, she hoped, some thoughts about them. Chateaubriand ignored this request. She then followed up with another letter, which was among those saved by Madame Recamier and published by her niece in 1860. In this second letter, dated June 14, 1825, Charlotte was sadly resigned to his indifference toward her requests, aware that she could not bring back the past and determined not to bother him again. The door was shut and sealed. Whatever had transpired between them was over.

Seeking to reconcile the facts about the relationship between Chateaubriand and Charlotte Ives with his moving descriptions of her in his memoirs was especially problematic given a letter that Chateaubriand scholar George Painter wrote to me on January 5, 1993, stating: "I have never, never found him positively untruthful in *Memoires d'outre-tombe,* despite his undeserved reputation and the efforts of others to find him so." One possible solution to the dilemma is to understand that Chateaubriand was likely using a familiar literary device, conflating one person with another, to protect or hide the identity of the person actually associated with the events. We can be reasonably sure that Chateaubriand met with my ancestor Thomas Fallon that London summer of 1822, given the rendering of the oil portrait of Thomas in all likelihood commissioned by Chateaubriand, shown in figure 9. The family story also maintains that, upon his departure, Chateaubriand gave his horse to Thomas as a gift. Since Chateaubriand had been meeting with Thomas, he would surely have met with Mary, mother of the young man whose education at a prestigious French college he had just sponsored. It was, after all, for her that he had taken the boy under his wing.

Mary, like Charlotte, had three sons. In Chateaubriand's account, Charlotte appears with just two of her sons, whom he estimates are sixteen and fourteen years old, but he does not mention whether they are her two younger sons or her two older ones. If these were Charlotte's two eldest sons, they would have been Samuel, who was fifteen at the time, and William, who was fourteen; alternatively, they could have been fourteen-year-old William accompanied by John, age twelve. But instead Mary could have been the subject of Chateaubriand's account, bringing her two sons whom he had not yet met—Cornelius, age sixteen, and Daniel, age ten.

Moreover, at least some of the loving vignettes and affectionate reminiscences that Chateaubriand attributes to his subsequent meetings with Charlotte very likely took place with Mary. The facts available to us are that Chateaubriand developed a deep and abiding commitment to Mary and her eldest son, Thomas, even supporting them financially over decades, and he chose to highlight in his memoirs only a superficial, almost childish romance with Charlotte. Perhaps, in recollections of his youth spent in exile, Chateaubriand merged these two lovely girls—one English, the other Irish—with his Sylphide into a single icon representing the wistful delirium of first love's enchantment.

If Chateaubriand and Mary were actually meeting in London during the summer of 1822, where was Mary's husband, Patrick? My family's oral history consistently recounts that Patrick left London for a few years to join a group of Irish patriots fighting alongside Simón Bolívar to free the South American colonies from Spanish rule,[7] although I have no documentary evidence to support this part of the story, and it is hard to imagine why a comfortably successful London merchant would head off on an exploit to undeveloped equatorial South America. Even so, given how much of my family's oral history has proven reliable, there is some prospect of this having occurred.

Simón Bolívar's revolutionary forces had begun to make substantial gains against the Spanish Crown around 1812. After 1814, however, the Franco-Spanish peninsular war had ended and Napoleon had been defeated, which permitted King Ferdinand

VII to deploy significant well-trained Spanish troops to battle the insurgents in South America. Responding in 1816, Bolívar authorized his deputy in London, Luis López Méndez, to help augment his army by recruiting volunteers to join the war of liberation. López Méndez successfully recruited Irishmen to this cause, with large numbers embarking for South America in the winter of 1817–1818, not to return until after the victory.[8] An expert estimated the number of Irish fighters in the Bolivarian forces at 3,650, constituting about 54 percent of all foreign fighters against the Spanish.[9] Their motives varied. Some went in hopes of material gain in the form of money and land; others sought adventure; and many had dreams of someday using their Bolivarian experience to achieve an independent Ireland. Bolívar's war for the independence of northern South America turned decisively in his favor with a victory in the Battle of Boyacá in late 1819, but the fighting continued and did not result in the dissolution of patriot armies until well into 1823. Thus, if Patrick Fallon participated in the battle for liberation of northern South America he would have left England around 1818 and returned around 1823.

In weaving together Mary's story with the possibility that Patrick was away during the summer of 1822, when Mary was seeing Chateaubriand, it is easy to surmise an impending tragedy. Upon his return, Patrick would have learned of the months-long companionship between his wife and the charismatic Frenchman, whereas up to that point he might have taken at face value a French nobleman's desire to assume the cost of educating the first son of the young woman who had aided him as an exiled émigré during his gravest hours. But reports of what had transpired between his wife and the viscount during the summer of 1822 may have broken Patrick's faith and put unbearable pressure on the marriage. In anger, he could have turned her out of the house.

With no secure refuge, Mary's first inclination may have been to turn to Chateaubriand for help. Well educated in an English school, she would have had a working command of the French language; and Paris could be reached readily from London. Once in Paris, she would likely have found that her friend and would-be protector was in no position to acknowledge her publicly but could provide occasional and likely ongoing financial support. As far-fetched as this account may seem, it aligns with facts that have been established.

Chateaubriand himself has told us more. In his desperate year of 1817, penniless and traveling with his wife, Céleste, from one generous host to another, Chateaubriand was moved by the song of a thrush in the woods, reminding him of his youth and initiating a resolve to pick up his pen and return to writing his memoirs. The episodes he subsequently recorded showed at the beginning of each chapter the date it was written. The account of his years as a young exile in London, from 1793 to 1800, was written between April and September of 1822, precisely the spring and summer he spent as ambassador in London.

Thus, we know that during the summer of 1822, when Chateaubriand was once more meeting with Charlotte and Mary, both now adults with memories of their own, he was shaping these women as girls in his memoirs. He wrote about watching the English schoolgirls passing by in a park in early fall 1793, causing him to be seized through the magic of his Sylphide by a "confusion of desire"; his stay in an attic garret in Marylebone; his flight to Beccles and sojourn with the Ives family in Bungay; his youthful romantic attraction to Charlotte; his escape from Bungay back to London; and his encounter with the beautiful tall Mary Neale at the home of Mrs. O'Leary on Hampstead Road.

It is clear in these episodes, as throughout his memoirs, that Chateaubriand was skillfully molding an account of his life experience, combining his present-day reflections with embellished images from his youthful past. As he was writing in summer 1822, he conspicuously featured Charlotte as a central character but, aside from the delicate and touching revelation of her by name as a beautiful young woman, wrote nothing about Mary. Now, from a distance of two hundred years beyond the narrative laid out by his pen on paper, we know that Mary and her son Thomas were central to his life story though absent from his memoirs. The most likely explanation for this discrepancy is that while his encounter with Charlotte was innocent enough to be safely chronicled, his extensive relationship with Mary and Thomas needed to remain hidden.

A hypothesis that explains this curious assemblage of facts is that four people suspected, probably believed, that Thomas was the son of Mary and Chateaubriand: Mary, Patrick, Chateaubriand, and Thomas. Patrick seems ultimately to have acted on this conviction, wanting nothing more to do with Mary and Thomas, banishing Mary, and turning his hat shop over to the second eldest son, Cornelius. Chateaubriand would not have been able to acknowledge his guarded and consequential relationship with Mary since he could not permit the conjecture that he had fathered a child out of wedlock to become public. Thomas, then in his twenties, had received an excellent education at a prestigious continental school, earning credentials superior to those of most of his peers and capable of pursuing any number of lucrative and satisfying careers in the British Isles. Yet, in his mid to late twenties, he was likely estranged from his father and perhaps disillusioned by Chateaubriand's treatment of his desperate mother.

Thomas, on the threshold of a beckoning adulthood, was left envisioning a continuing future in Great Britain or France with more despondency than promise. Therefore, after learning of the death of his mother in the late 1820s, he chose a solitary adventure, leaving for the jungles of South America. It was the most remote and forbidding place an educated young European could imagine, while at the same time its allure, as "the New World," augured for an intellectual an unconstrained launch into a mysteriously fascinating future. Since Thomas, as a student, had surely admired Chateaubriand, his choice of a life in the Americas may well have been modeled after Chateaubriand's own adventures, even though Thomas, unlike his benefactor, never returned to Europe.

As much as Chateaubriand might have wanted to memorialize his relationship with Mary in his memoirs, he could not, for reasons of propriety and legality. Instead, presumptively, he conflated Mary with Charlotte, hiding Mary from view but expressing his love for her in free-flowing verse alluding to Charlotte. This was likely his stratagem to avoid facing uncomfortable questions about ostensible paternity. It might also have reflected an effort to protect Mary and Thomas by preventing their story from intersecting with his own.

Can we know who was actually the father of Thomas? There are only two circumstances by which Chateaubriand could have become the father of Thomas without the contemporaneous knowledge of Mary's husband, Patrick. First, after an intimate encounter in 1798, Mary could have missed a menstrual period in January 1799. Chateaubriand, a married man with hopes of fame in France, could not marry her. His next best option would have been to help her find a respectable Catholic husband with a secure income. Chateaubriand and Patrick were, in fact, the same age, about ten years older than Mary. The two men probably moved in the same circles, composed of French and Irish Catholics seeking to exercise their religious culture in an unwelcoming London. With Chateaubriand's assistance, Mary could then have become Patrick's friend, capturing him in marriage the old-fashioned way.

The other possibility supportive of Chateaubriand's paternity would have been that Mary and Patrick had become a couple and planned the marriage that took place in early March 1799. During this time, or even after the marriage, Mary may have had occasional meetings with Chateaubriand, at least one of which might have culminated in a physically intimate encounter. As singularly emotional, even criminal, as the sin of adultery would have been to the lovers, it is nonetheless a possibility not beyond the experience of other Londoners of the day.

It is hard to imagine what people in the early nineteenth century understood about the temporal relation between coitus and birth. The causal association between the two events was well understood, of course, but how it all worked was still a mystery, and details, such as the length of gestation, leaned heavily on clumsy guesswork. Male spermatozoa had been discovered in the late seventeenth century by a Dutch scientist, Antonie van Leeuwenhoek. In the male-dominated world of science, most physicians thought the full child was contained as a homunculus in the head of the sperm cell. The female ovum was not discovered until 1827, by German scientist Karl Ernst von Baer, and not until 1876 did another German scientist, Oscar Hertwig, prove that conception was due to fusion of an ovum and sperm cell.

A standard average period of human gestation—280 days from the beginning of the last menstrual period—was initially set forth in 1804 by one of the first physicians to specialize in obstetrics, a German named Franz Karl Naegele. Even after this roughly nine-month interval became accepted as a norm it was understood that women individually experienced substantial variation in gestation times. Given the uncertainty in the late eighteenth century about the biology of childbirth, even a single intimate encounter between Mary and Chateaubriand from late

1798 through the first several months of 1799 would have given them reason to regard Thomas as their child.

Unfortunately, I have still not been able to find a reliable birth date for Thomas. The December 1818 passport I discovered states his age as eighteen, implying he was born in 1800. But he could have been born earlier, so much so that to avoid embarrassment Patrick and Mary might have assigned a later birthday in 1800. If Mary became pregnant after her wedding day, the infant could have been born in the last weeks of 1799 or early in 1800. We know that Chateaubriand did not end his exile in England and return to France until May 1800, late enough for him to have witnessed Thomas as an infant before leaving London.

I was asked once during a visit to France if I might provide a DNA sample that could perhaps be compared with samples taken from male descendants of Chateaubriand's uncles or with an extant lock of hair from Chateaubriand himself. The conversation was pure conjecture, and I brushed it aside since it seemed unnecessarily cumbersome and embarrassing, even arrogant. Nonetheless, after I returned home the idea germinated, as it posed a resolution to the stubborn question concerning the paternity of Thomas. The appeal of this line of investigation was even more enticing to me because the technology was so new, having only recently become available commercially. I realized then that I could circumvent the involvement of anyone in France by directly exploring my own genetic past.

Today, genetic technology that was unimaginable at the beginning of the nineteenth century can verify lines of ancient paternity. Through contemporary DNA analysis, a study of the Y chromosome reveals lineage from father to father, indefinitely to all previous fathers, thus locating paternal ancestry in the distant past. Consequently I excitedly ordered DNA tests from three newly established commercial companies. The first sample I sent for analysis suggested a recent Irish ancestry but did not rule out ancestry from Brittany. The Bretons, like the Irish, were Celts, with common ancestry dating back to about 300 CE. Both groups would likely have similar DNA. So I sought a second analysis from a company with a large public database and a third sample from a company specializing in autosomal analysis. The results of the second and third tests reinforced those of the first test, pointing more definitively to Irish ancestry and, particularly, to County Roscommon in north-central Ireland, the ancestral home of the Fallon clan.

What is more, a public genetic database identified two individuals with my surname Fallon, both previously unknown to me, with whom my Y chromosome proved we shared a common ancestor. One of them confirmed to me that he had recent ancestors from County Roscommon; the probability that we share an ancestor within the past eight generations exceeds .67. For either of these two men, the probability of my sharing the same ancestor exceeds .99 after eighteen generations. Since analysis of my DNA proves I share paternal ancestry with men named Fallon, I cannot share paternal ancestry with men named Chateaubriand, leading me at last to conclude that Thomas was, in fact, the biological son of Mary Neale and Patrick Fallon. This discovery, emerging from my own body, caps my investigative journey with a powerful lesson: what we believe, or what we wish for, has far greater impact on our motives and decisions than reason alone. This must have been true for Mary and Chateaubriand.

In the late eighteenth and early nineteenth centuries, contraceptive methods were primitive and unreliable. A man who had intimate encounters with numerous women normally fathered several children. Chateaubriand was such a man. Ever since his coming of age with Lucile in Combourg, he sought and was rewarded by the companionship of numerous women, attracted as he was by humanity of a different gender, the richness of shared ideas, and mysteries of desire. Even masculine vanity played a role. For example, in fall 1799, while Mary was pregnant with Thomas, Chateaubriand competed with another French émigré for the affection of a vivacious young woman who had recently arrived in London from a plantation in the Caribbean, Henriette de Belloy, and he proudly won.

Given his proclivities involving women, we would expect Chateaubriand to have fathered many children or none at all. It defies logic to imagine that he would have had just one child. The higher probability is that Chateaubriand was infertile. A man of colossal ambition, strong enough to have craved a son, his life's journey denied him the thrill of holding his own infant in his arms. While affected by romantic feelings for Charlotte and Mary, between 1793 and 1801 his imagination drove him to write the fable *Atala*, which curiously includes multiple accounts of lifeless infants, either just deceased or soon to be conceived, whose souls are thought to continue enraptured existence through the thwarted motherhood of maidens who, despite their loss, pay honor to the deceased infants in stylized rituals. Since these descriptions of dead babies do not seem to advance his narrative, they remain a puzzle for literary analysts. It is possible that the author, whose life in exile at the time was enlivened by romance with two very different young women, neither of whom he could marry, was haunted by thoughts of forfeited fatherhood and thus preoccupied with the souls of lost infants.

This account of Chateaubriand's relationship to Mary Neale Fallon is consistent with the available facts, many of which have only come to light through discoveries in the course of my quest in recent decades. Further investigation may support this interpretation or force the telling of a different tale. Confronting one conundrum after another, my rendition asserts that the calamity that befell Mary, that drove my great-great-grandfather to the New World, and that led Chateaubriand to hide from view some of the most significant people in his life was caused by his persistently gnawing submission to an irresistible but forbidden love, fueled by the searing power of imaginative longing. If the son Chateaubriand fervently sought to embrace was not biologically Thomas, the boy was nonetheless a fitting avatar for what a son might have been, a lost soul brought to life by an honored and honoring mother.

Whether Chateaubriand acknowledged regret about his involvement with Mary and Thomas presents a final conundrum. There are clues that he did. Toward the end of his reminiscences of exile in his memoirs, Chateaubriand penned a short chapter entitled "A Defect of My Character." He noted at the top of the chapter that it was first written in summer 1822, at the time he delicately mentioned Mary and described his encounters with Charlotte. He later added another note indicating that he edited it in 1846, two years before his death, intimating its importance to him. It was an unusual interjection in which he mused about his propensity for reserved behavior that caused him not to be forthright or transparent. He wrote that he was a man of passion with little evidence of such raging emotions in his outward demeanor. He asserted that his reserve with others had led him to refrain from behaving as he should have. For example, Chateaubriand pointed to the many times that Mrs. Ives, Charlotte's mother, inquired about his family, providing him with multiple opportunities to disclose that he was married. Yet he remained silent, he wrote, holding his thoughts at bay, while aware on some level that he should have spoken about Céleste. He admitted his reticence had provoked a disaster that could have been avoided.

Chateaubriand made a point of revealing something important in this chapter, with a final revision late in his waning years, about the danger that lurks in hiding uncomfortable truths in hopes they may never surface, not even to avert foreseeable tragedy. He was describing guilt, which is also what he signaled when he acknowledged Mary's insight in discerning some heart wound of his, as she peered deeply through his eyes into his soul, perceiving the intensity of his conflicted pathos at Mrs. O'Leary's fateful tea party. Chateaubriand reacted to Mary's perspicacity with what seems an expression of remorse, a true rarity for this carefully staged author, by confessing, "I carried my heart I know not how."

CHAPTER 6

Tracking
the Legacy

LEGACY ENDURES.

Chateaubriand was swift in his sponsorship of Thomas, arranging his entry into a prestigious collège royal, taking responsibility for his oversight, and assuring full financial support. He thus laid upon Thomas the foundation of a personal legacy springing from his affection for the boy and his mother. That legacy of his love has endured for more than two centuries. In fact, Chateaubriand's contribution to my genetic history, had it occurred, would have amounted to a minuscule fraction of my ancestral gene pool. It was his behavior, not his genes, that had a profound effect on my life. He was the agent who had endowed Thomas with the intellectual capital propelling successful life choices, character, and skills.

Chateaubriand thus tweaked the arc of ancestry impacting all of Thomas Fallon's descendants, providing a lasting legacy of his debt to Mary and his care for Thomas.

Beyond Thomas, there is sadness, even tragedy, in the fate of his mother, Mary Neale. I came to love her as part of a happy story about her role in helping Chateaubriand. My quest revealed, however, that the family oral history recounted only the tender part of the story, leaving unsaid—perhaps unknown or forgotten—the unspeakable heartache over her lonely demise in a foreign country, apparently spurned by the powerful man she came to treasure above all others. Chateaubriand certainly loved Mary, at least for a time, but what Mary likely did not sense was his inability to give his heart unconditionally to anyone beyond the moment of his infatuation. There were long-term dimensions of love in their relationship, shown in large part by Chateaubriand's affectionate letter of 1817 to Thomas upon the boy's arrival in Amiens, which Thomas treasured enough to save, and has thus survived for two hundred years.

There is little evidence of relations between Chateaubriand and Mary during his five-month return to London in 1822, but it is plausible to speculate that a spark of lingering love still glowed between them that summer. The next we learn of Mary is of her destitute condition in Paris four years later, when Chateaubriand instructs his financial agent to give her money from time to time. This is the legacy Chateaubriand has left me. It is a legacy of convoluted love, delivered tangibly through education of my great-great-grandfather, Thomas, who benefited immensely from this endowment, valued highly what it meant for its own sake, and put it to good use.

It is natural to wonder where we came from, even though the ability to successfully navigate life does not depend upon knowledge of our personal ancestry. The novelist James Michener, for example, was a foundling, discovered as a swaddled infant on a doorstep in a tiny town in Bucks County, Pennsylvania. He was adopted by an impoverished widow named Mabel Michener, in whose loving home he grew up as an only child in extreme poverty. In his adulthood, he treated strangers with respect because he imagined that anyone he saw from a distance or met personally might be a blood relative. It surely is no accident that his novels portray families as they descend from generation to generation over many lifetimes. Michener knew that ancestry was a special kind of personal history, perhaps because he would never know his own.

I don't know how I would have been affected had I learned that the eminent Chateaubriand was a direct ancestor of mine. In the end it doesn't matter, as I am five generations removed from Mary Neale and Patrick Fallon, with four pairs of parents on the paternal line, as well as an equal number on the maternal, producing families between those two and me. It is enough to live life as we find it, moving forward, as was the path taken by James Michener, who understood that ignorance of genetic history did not remove him from the human family. Michener realized that knowing personal stories about people who lived before us, whether biological relatives or strangers, can be a powerful force in shaping our own identity. Such stories, relating an arresting human history of respect, conflict, wonder, and regret, enrich our understanding of ourselves. They feed our imaginations, helping us see our places in the world more fully, just as my quest, culminating in discovery of Chateaubriand's story, has changed how I think about myself and my ancestry.

My ancestors left me with documents and tales that trace their history from Europe to America through colorful episodes, each with lessons that continue to influence their descendants. Listening to my father opened a palpable lifeline to what turned out to be a surprisingly heartrending story of Mary Eliza Neale. This recent journey of discovery began with a tale about an Irish girl who met a sick and impoverished French gentleman in a park in London and aided him in his time of need, in return for which the gentleman, who became an esteemed writer and famed public personality, ensured the superior education of her son. Those events must have been later recounted by the boy, Thomas, to his own son, Diego, then carried over four generations to reach me. Tracking the stations along that route illuminates how Chateaubriand's legacy of love expanded over generations, increasingly fostering successful lives in the New World of the Americas.

The chronicle begins with Thomas, who was probably at odds with his father when, late in the 1820s, he learned of his mother's death in Paris. He was ready for a new start in life and ripe for adventure, perhaps inspired in part by Chateaubriand's own escapades in the New World. Capitalizing on the success of the revolutionaries in South America, some groups of British speculators sought to exploit the assets left behind by the Spanish. One of these, incorporating itself as the Colombian Mining Association of London, was devoted to extracting mineral wealth from South America. Through a newspaper ad, Thomas learned of the association's search for a director of mining operations in the heavily forested village of Santa Ana, near the equator in Tolima Province, Colombia, site of a lucrative silver mine. Thomas applied, was accepted, and left for the New World before the end of the decade.

Arriving in Santa Ana, Thomas followed in the footsteps of the mine's first English director, Robert Stephenson, who had returned to England to help his father, George, with crucial modifications on the Rocket, the first successful steam locomotive in England. Robert Stephenson went on to become the most esteemed engineer of the Victorian industrial revolution and is today the only engineer so honored by burial in Westminster Abbey. Like Stephenson before him, Thomas contracted malaria soon after his arrival in Santa Ana. In a delirium, he was carried off to what my father called "the great house" in the nearby town of Mariquita, where he was nursed back to health by the beautiful and compassionate Marcela Carrión de León y Armero, who had similarly tended Stephenson.

When his health returned, Thomas, like Stephenson, proposed marriage to Marcela. She had sweetly and politely rejected Stephenson's proposal, but accepted Thomas's. They were married around 1831 and had three children: Tomasa in 1832, Diego in 1834, and Cornelia in 1836. Although Marcela had named their first child after him, their other children bore the names of his brothers, who were an important part of his life. Their second child, Diego, was named after James (the English equivalent of Diego), whom I suspect died in childhood, and their third child was named after Cornelius.

Thomas went on to become director of all mining operations in the nascent Republic of Colombia. Those he supervised most closely were the salt mines in Zipaquirá, the coal mines in Nemocón, the gold and silver mines in Santa Ana, and the emerald mines in Muzo. He arranged for Diego to be educated by Jesuits, who soon recognized in him a precocious, enthusiastic student. In 1849, a violent change in the Colombian government resulted in expulsion of the Jesuits, who, as was well known, read books and were therefore not tolerated by dictators. This interruption in Diego's education created a crisis for the fifteen-year-old, but Marcela intervened. She had been told, when parting from Stephenson, that she could rely on him to ensure for her future children a proper English education. So with Marcela's encouragement Thomas sent a letter to his brother Cornelius with instructions to hand deliver it to Stephenson.

Stephenson's reply—handed down by my forebears and given to me by my father—is written in a handsome Victorian hand from his residence at 24 Great George Street, London, and dated August 21, 1850. Thomas's handwriting is visible at the top, underlined, with the notation: "<u>Muzo, November 2 = 71 days.</u>" The letter begins: "A few days ago I received your letter dated 3d of June from your brother and this morning I received the beautiful present from Marcela, for which I beg you to return my sincere thanks." Stephenson then wrote about his professional life as an engineer, contrasting it with Thomas's career at the silver mine and wishing him well:

> Now with respect to your son Diego, if he should come to England you may rely upon my aiding him in every way in my power for the sake of his mother....When your son arrives you may rest assured that I will do my best and confer with your brother and if I see my way I shall endeavor to contribute towards his education by relieving you of some portion of the expense....I shall have pleasure in doing the same for the son of Marcela by way of proving that I have not forgotten the days I spent and those I knew in Mariquita.

Thomas and Marcela wasted no time getting young Diego off to England, nearly replicating Mary and Patrick's response following Chateaubriand's gift to Thomas. In the former case, Thomas was sent to a foreign country to obtain a fine education he couldn't receive at home, supported by a famous person who once loved his mother. In the latter case, Diego was sent to a foreign country to obtain a fine education he couldn't receive at home, supported by a famous person who once loved his mother.

Diego arrived on the ship *Victoria* at the Port of London on Saturday, November 23, 1850, according to the official record of alien arrivals. Stephenson immediately enrolled him in an excellent secondary school in London, but Diego complained that it was insufficiently religious, so Stephenson then arranged for him to be enrolled at Stonyhurst College, the famous Jesuit educational complex in Lancashire. A school register from 1851 shows Diego enrolled as James Fallon, scholar from New Granada. Not far from the school is the Lake District, where Diego became deeply influenced by the romantic English lake poets Wordsworth, Coleridge, and Southey. After receiving his diploma from Stonyhurst, Diego enrolled at a technical college in Newcastle, a school Stephenson had earlier attended, having been born and raised in that city. Diego graduated in due course with credentials qualifying him as a mechanical engineer with a specialization in railways. He was at the same time a multitalented romantic at the height of the romantic movement, playing violin and piano in salon society to support himself, and writing poetry.

In 1852, Thomas and Marcela sent their daughters Tomasa and Cornelia to an Ursuline Academy in Paris for a secondary education, called at the time a finishing school. In doing so, Thomas once more paid forward the gift from Chateaubriand. Courtesy of the renowned French writer, Thomas had experienced the value of a first-class education and, even in remote undeveloped regions of former Spanish colonies in the New World, made extraordinary efforts to secure excellent European educations for his own children.

In early 1858, Tomasa contracted typhoid fever and died in Paris. Diego went to Paris to oversee burial arrangements and to comfort Cornelia, who remained in Paris until the end of that school year, coming to England in late May to join her brother at Stephenson's home. Diego had just received a commission to design and oversee the construction of Spain's first railway between Barcelona and Madrid. As summer progressed, Cornelia became increasingly sick. Stephenson's physician told Diego, "The best thing you can do for this girl is get her home." Diego canceled his contract with the Spanish government and, in October 1858, set forth with Cornelia for Colombia. As they left Liverpool, Diego began a pencil sketch of his sister. A few days later Cornelia died in his arms on the high seas. Diego bartered with the captain for permission to keep her remains on board until the first landfall, which is where she was finally buried. Her grave, unmarked, lies on a small island in the bay off Saint Thomas, in the Virgin Islands.

In his personal journal, Diego started a letter to an English school friend, describing his journey home, recounting how the moment his feet touched Colombia's shore at Barranquilla he breathed the sweet air and knew he was where destiny had intended him to be. Able to identify various species of birds through their birdsong, he reveled in hearing his free-flying companions, especially those that mated for life. The draft of his letter continues:

I have been wandering about "my old familiar places" in this country...passing the nights in Dreams of England... and waking amidst forest and mountains with the cries of the wild birds above and the roar of native torrents around me. When I arrived in Bogotá, I was visited by my friends in mourning for three days; then I proceeded to the emerald mines where my father and mother were staying. They had already received my letter informing them of the death of Cornelia.

The road to the mines is in two or three points crossed by fearfully rapid and large rivers, over which are suspended bridges made of creeping plants, in the chain bridge style, which are pretty strong for one or two persons, but not enough for mules. These lands, the Muzo, are considered by naturalists amongst the most fertile in the world. They produce emeralds, the most beautiful species of the butterfly kind, the best coffee in South America, very aromatic tobacco, and to crown its merits it possesses a small bird gifted with a divine musical genius as well as with the sweetest and at the same time one of the loudest voices of the winged creation.

At seven o'clock at night I arrived at the mine. My father was standing on the top of the hills. I embraced him. He wept a little, and we then proceeded to the house and embraced my mother who cried for a long time. I referred to them the peaceful and angelic death of Cornelia and they received consolation. I passed three months comfortably with my parents in this recess far far away from all the world.

After his arrival, Diego presented his parents with the pencil sketch he had completed of Cornelia (see figure 13), which has become an iconic family heirloom.

A little more than four years later, in spring 1863, Thomas died suddenly of a heart attack. Marcela followed within three months, dying of a broken heart. Diego, at age twenty-nine, was now the sole surviving Fallon in Colombia. At a social gathering in the mining village of Nemocón, Diego was smitten by a young woman called "La Estrella," whose name was Amalia Luque de Lizarralde. Following his heart, he sought her out while she was alone in the kitchen and declared, "Should you ever desire to embark upon marriage, I trust it will be with me!" They were married on October 6, 1866, in Nemocón.

Although Diego was a qualified engineer who had designed a successful crop harvester, he abandoned the profession, settling with Amalia in Candelaria, the cobblestoned heart of Bogotá, and hanging outside the door a shingle inscribed: "Diego Fallon, Professor of Music, Languages, and Mathematics." Supporting himself as a freelance instructor, he also composed poems that won praise from romantic Colombians. His best known poem, "La Luna," was said by *bogotanos* to be the most perfect verse on the subject of the moon written in the Castilian language. Some of his other poems, such as "Las Rocas de Suesca," "En la Montaña," "La Palma en el Desierto," and "Mintamos," established his reputation as being among the antecedents of the literary style called magical realism. Diego's uncanny ability to subject complex themes and profound wording to the strict discipline of meter and rhyme earned him recognition as a Colombian example of the French literary movement Parnassianism.

He remained a devout Catholic throughout his life, much like Chateaubriand, perhaps even inspired by him. On August 13, 1905, Diego Fallon died in Bogotá. In 1930, the municipality of the mining village of Santa Ana, where Diego was born, legally renamed itself Falan in his honor. In 1984, on the 150th anniversary of his birth, the Republic of Colombia issued a postage stamp depicting his image, illuminated by a moon above his shoulder (see figure 14).

Diego and Amalia's long and happy marriage produced four children, two boys and two girls (see figure 15). Cornelia, born in 1867, remained single, earning a reputation as disciplinary family matriarch. Luís Tomás, born in 1869, pursued a career as a professor in Bogotá. María, born in 1873, married a businessman, Nelson Gnecco from Riohacha, the hometown of Gabriel García Márquez, and resided with him prosperously in Bogotá. The youngest was my grandfather, Diego José, born in 1877 and called Dieguito by his parents.

One day after Mass, Diego José found himself following a beautiful woman leaving the cathedral. When she noticed, he awkwardly introduced himself. Blanca Convers de Codazzi had earlier hoped to pursue a religious life as a nun but had been counseled to doubt this vocation by the mother superior of the local convent. Blanca saw in the vulnerable Diego José a new life project. They were married on April 21, 1907, in Bogotá. Their three children were my father, Carlos, born in 1909; his brother, Eduardo, born in 1912; and a sister, María Elena, called Marelen, born in 1917. My father always claimed he had been born twice. The first time was in the Quinta de Bolívar, the historic home in the heart of Bogotá that "the liberator," Simón Bolívar, had used as his headquarters and where Diego José was a curator and became father to a newborn son named Carlos, who died a few weeks after birth. My father told me he just wasn't ready. The second time was in a house on 16th Street in Candelaria, where my father, also named Carlos, greeted the world with happiness and curiosity.

Diego José, like his father, was a gregarious and engaging storyteller, a beloved socialite among *bogotano* families. Doña Blanca believed he was living on rays cast by his father's star and thus robbed of personal ambition; to rectify this deficiency, in 1922 she used her influence in the government to secure him an appointment as Colombian consul to the United States in New Orleans. Once there, Diego José found his eldest son, Carlos, an unmanageable enigma because of his penchant for escapades that brought him into conflict with authorities, especially those in the Church. Therefore, Diego José made good on a threat to discipline Carlos by sending him to a monastery in Barcelona, Spain, to study for the priesthood.

After Carlos completed eighth grade, which was the highest grade offered in the tax-supported public schools of New Orleans in 1923, Doña Blanca was charged with taking Carlos to the port, where he was to embark for the monastery in Barcelona. On the bright morning of his departure, as they walked toward the Mississippi River she asked him, while looking straight ahead, "Do you really want to be a priest?"

"No, Mamá," he answered, "I'd much rather be a sailor!"

She carried a velvet purse with silver coins intended for his tuition at the monastery. When mother and son reached the ship, she sought out the captain and, as was her way, gave him a commanding instruction: "Please take this boy and make him a sailor. If you succeed, you may keep the money in this purse. If you fail, you must turn the boy and the purse over to the priests who will be waiting for him in Barcelona." With that, fourteen-year-old Carlos became a sailor and found that he loved the sea and the people who plied it (see figure 16). It took several days for Blanca to explain to Diego José that Carlos was likely to end up on a boat rather than in a seminary, and still longer for Diego José to write to the monastery. As a result, when the five-masted sailing ship arrived in port, the priests had not yet been informed of a possible change in plans. One morning the captain called Carlos over and explained that the finial on top of the mainmast, a black globe, was decorated with gold-leaf filigree and needed to be touched up. Upon being sent aloft, Carlos, clinging to the mast while painting, observed three black-robed figures boarding the ship. He could not hear the conversation, but he could see the captain, with shrugged shoulders and arms splayed wide, indicating in a raised voice that he could not confirm what the robed men wanted. After looking around, they left the ship, and the captain signaled that Carlos could now descend, as the priests had been turned away. After many adventures sailing the world, including being kidnapped for eighteen months in China by the warlord of the north, Chang Tso-lin, Carlos returned to Colombia for his required military training.

Upon completing his military requirements, Carlos returned by ship from Barranquilla to his parents' home in New Orleans. Carlos was an avid reader throughout his life, but his library while at sea was mostly confined to the books available on shipboard, leading to an unusual education. On the vessel departing from Barranquilla, he came upon a book by Lord Baden-Powell, founder of the Boy Scouts, which convinced him that the scouts were a paramilitary organization, an idea he found inspirational. Therefore, after arriving at his parents' home Carlos organized a Boy Scout troop, whose exploits soon garnered attention throughout the city. Through that organization, he met my mother, Maureen Byrne, who was the older sister of one of his scouts. Carlos was twenty-one years old, and she was fourteen.

On Maureen's sixteenth birthday, in 1931, Carlos presented her with a diamond engagement ring, which he had financed by rum-running from Cuba since the abolition amendment was still in effect. By then, the Great Depression had reached New Orleans, where work could no longer be found. So when he was offered a job by the Colombian Coffee Growers Association in New York, he added Maureen to his savings account at Seamen's Bank in New Orleans and left for New York. Maureen graduated early from high school, found a job as a secretary, and from her weekly income was able to give her parents cash for the household, leaving her with a small remainder to deposit in the savings account, which was augmented by funds Carlos sent to the bank by mail.

Carlos mailed Maureen three letters every week, the last by special delivery, carried by a boy on a bicycle who rang his handlebar bell as he approached the house on North Johnson Street where Maureen's immediate and distant family members were residing together to economize. My mother's family was descended primarily from French immigrants. Her grandparents, referred to as Mamou and Papou, spoke almost exclusively creole French; and Maureen could trace her ancestry, via her maternal grandfather, Joseph A. E. Livaudais, back to the sixteenth century in, of all places, Saint-Malo.

While Carlos was working in New York, in Colombia's southernmost village of Leticia a border war broke out between Colombia and Peru over territory around the headwaters of the Amazon River. The Colombian military knew the war had to be fought largely on waterways and that with no functional navy they would have to create one. During his military training, Carlos had impressed the top brass with his expertise on ships; consequently, he was contacted and given secret orders to buy a yacht at the Brooklyn Navy Yard, convert it into a gunship, recruit a Colombian crew off the streets of New York, sail through the Caribbean Sea then up the Amazon River, and start shooting at Peruvians. This excited my twenty-three-year-old father, who executed the orders brilliantly, having managed to recruit marines, assemble a flotilla of ships, and, by age twenty-nine, be appointed commander in chief of what became, mostly as a result of his efforts, the Colombian Navy.

In the meantime, Maureen's father had found a job in Houston, where the family had relocated. Carlos was still writing letters to her three times weekly, although, coming from the Amazon jungle, they were delivered erratically. In late December 1933, however, the letters stopped altogether, causing Maureen to worry. Toward the end of January, a letter from Carlos finally arrived, but the handwriting was uneven and lacking the confident strokes to which she had become accustomed.

In the letter, Carlos reported that he had come down with malaria, had been delirious, and had to be transported by soldiers and pack burros to a hospital on the savanna of Bogotá, where he now was. He explained that he was also afflicted with beriberi, a nutritional disease affecting his knees. He told her his feelings for her had not changed—he had always intended to return to the United States, marry her, and start a family—but now he feared the United States would not give him a visa because of his disease and his military service to Colombia; nor would the Colombian government let him go because he was vital to their war effort. All of this, he said, made his imminent return unlikely, which was unfair to her. Although he still loved her, he wanted her to know that she should consider herself free to think of others.

After reading the letter, Maureen took matters into her own hands. Without informing her parents but with resolute purpose, the eighteen-year-old left the house right away, took a bus to the Western Union office in downtown Houston, and sent Carlos a telegram. It contained just nine words: "You stay put. I'm coming down. We're getting married." By this time, there was enough money in their joint savings account for her to purchase a one-way ticket to Colombia on a United Fruit Company steamer. She celebrated her nineteenth birthday going through the Panama Canal. Maureen and Carlos were married in the Chapinero neighborhood of Bogotá on June 16, 1934. I was born in 1938 in Cartagena, where the fleet was stationed; and my sister, Patricia, was born there in 1939. In 1940, we immigrated as a family to Chicago, where Diego José was then serving as Colombian consul.

In several ways, my father's life paralleled that of Chateaubriand. Both received formal schooling until age fourteen, when they left to follow the call of the sea, that profound aquatic expanse each of them found alluring. But whereas Chateaubriand's hopes were thwarted by state politics, Carlos succeeded through luck and enthusiasm. And although the aristocratic Frenchman had a more formal academic background than the Colombian youth, both adventurers valued knowledge so highly that they read deeply and continually and mastered multiple modern and ancient languages, routinely applying what they learned to the world as they found it. The tale of Chateaubriand tied to a mast during a storm at sea reminded me of my father describing the churning sea as a challenging friend whose seemingly irregular movements came to be understood and anticipated by experienced sailors. Both men continually reinvented themselves as the times required, their lives becoming works of art.

These family stories in skeletal form trace the path between Mary Neale and me. Other living descendants of Thomas Fallon include my sister, Pat Fallon, an artist residing in Cleveland; my children and hers; and scores of cousins descended from the line begun by the poet Diego Fallon and his wife, Amalia Luque. Many live in Colombia, while others live in Spain and in the United States, especially the Miami area.

Upon encountering my family history, Chateaubriand authority Pierre Riberette was struck by the many similarities to Chateaubriand's life he found reflected in the lives of contemporary descendants of Thomas Fallon. Among them are diplomats, such as a recent president of Colombia, Ernesto Samper, now living in Spain; a leading writer and satirist, Daniel Samper, also living in Spain; an influential architect, Germán Samper, whose work has been exhibited in the Museum of Modern Art in New York; an established poet and professor at the University of Miami, Luís Carlos Fallon; a physician in Florida, Diego Fallon; a clinical psychologist in Florida, Miguel Firpi; CEO of the Wildlife Conservation Society in New York, Cristián Samper; a renowned environmentalist, Mauricio Gnecco; and at least one gregarious storytelling nun in Colombia, Lizzy Fallon. For an example straight out of *Atala* or *René*, there is also Diego Samper-Martinez, an artist who has established an ecological tourist lodge, Calanoa, in the wilderness along the banks of the Upper Amazon River, in close cooperation with the neighboring indigenous Mocagua people.

Given enough descendants, it is possible to cherry pick those who share characteristics with a presumed ancestor. Common sense, however, demands that we recognize the role of chance and coincidence when engaged in an exercise like this because, for example, we know from my long quest that Chateaubriand was not a biological ancestor of the cousins I have in common with Thomas. Nonetheless, whether or not the direct descendants of Thomas Fallon are aware of the legacy of their ancestry, to the degree that their life outcomes depended on education, many have enjoyed the fruits of Chateaubriand's investment in Thomas.

The searing truth I have learned while following the gossamer threads of ancestry left to me by my father is that Chateaubriand in fact bequeathed to our family a legacy inspired by love. His gift of a first-class education for Thomas was surely the Frenchman's delivery on a promise made to the boy's mother, who, while rescuing him from near death when he was in perilous exile, had won his heart. A perhaps less obvious gift inspired by Chateaubriand's tangled love for Thomas's mother was the spirit of adventure instilled in the boy at a young age, awakening within him a remarkable resilience.

Just as Chateaubriand's love-infused legacy was secured through Thomas, Mary's was no less, expressed early on through her loving, compassionate aid to Chateaubriand and subsequently through her enduring role in family lore as mother and feminine spirit. The enchanting story of the girl in the park and her miraculous intervention on behalf of the starving French aristocrat has left an indelible mark on our family heritage, despite her presumptively sad end, hardly a trace of which mars the sweet memory of her younger years.

Ultimately, Chateaubriand's investment in Mary's eldest son immensely increased the prospects of success not only for Thomas but for countless future generations. Without his charity to Thomas, I would not be who I am. I was able to become a successful academician because of the intellect he nurtured in Thomas, which Thomas paid forward to his son, Diego, and which Diego then paid forward to his children, yielding benefits that continue to multiply as each new generation crafts its own future.

The descendants of Thomas Fallon owe a large debt to the life-affirming, adventurous, creative spirit of François-René Chateaubriand. Despite his crafted complaint about a melancholy life having been inflicted upon him, he was governed by a charitable heart that carried him, even if he knew not how he carried it. His was a heart with enough courage and compassion to provide the eldest son of Mary Neale and Patrick Fallon an education destined to brighten many subsequent lives in the New World.

Chateaubriand saw the world beyond the Atlantic Ocean as strange, ripe with possibility, alive with magic, unleashing the dilemmas and joys of the human spirit in unencumbered innocence, reflecting his own yearning. He set his two popular novellas, *Atala* and *René*, in such a world, conjured as free of many of Europe's complications.

Today, Chateaubriand's mortal remains lie gazing across the sea, surely fixed on that land of his imagination. His lasting legacy of love—the grace it gave to Thomas Fallon—would forever endure in the New World.

If he only knew. If Mary only knew. We are here. We are grateful.

Notes

Citations from Chateaubriand's *Mémoires d'outre-tombe* (MOT) contain the official text in electronic form obtained from the Bibliothèque Nationale de France (http://www.bnf.fr/), showing volume (*livre*), chapter (*chapitre*), and page numbers.

Preface

1. Daniel Fallon, "À la Recherche d'un Fils de Chateaubriand," *Société Chateaubriand, Bulletin Année* 38 (1996): 13–22.

2. Daniel Fallon, "Retours au Pays," in *Chateaubriand 98*, ed. Jacques Gury (Rennes, France: Institut Culturel de Bretagne, 1999), 103–105.

3. François-René de Chateaubriand, *Memoirs from Beyond the Grave: 1768–1800*, trans. Alex Andriesse (New York: *New York Review of Books*, 2018); François-René de Chateaubriand, *Memoirs from Beyond the Tomb*, trans. Robert Baldick (London: Penguin, 2014).

Chapter 1

1. Carlos Fallon, *Value Analysis to Improve Productivity* (New York: John Wiley & Sons, 1971).

2. Carlos Fallon, *A Variety of Fallon* (Boston: Little, Brown, 1950), 44–52.

Chapter 2

1. Mon père commençait alors une promenade, qui necessait qu'à l'heure de son coucher. Il était vêtu d'une robe de ratine blanche, ou plutôt d'une espèce de manteau que je n'ai vu qu'à lui. Sa tête, demi-chauve, était couverte d'un grand bonnet blanc

qui se tenait tout droit. Lorsqu'en se promenant, il s'éloignait du foyer, la vaste salle était si peu éclairée par une seule bougie qu'on ne le voyait plus; on l'entendait seulement encore marcher dans les ténèbres: puis il revenait lentement vers la lumière et émergeait peu à peu de l'obscurité, comme un spectre, avec sa robe blanche, son bonnet blanc, sa figure longue et pâle. Lucile et moi, nous échangions quelques mots à voix basse, quand il était à l'autre bout de la salle; nous nous taisions quand il se rapprochait de nous. Il nous disait, en passant: "De quoi parliez-vous?" Saisis de terreur, nous ne répondions rien; il continuait sa marche. Le reste de la soirée, l'oreille n'était plus frappée que du bruit mesuré de ses pas, des soupirs de ma mère et du murmure du vent. (MOT, livre 3, chapitre 3, 68–69.)

2. François-René de Chateaubriand, *René: Textes Littéraires Français, Texte de l'Édition de 1805* (Geneva: Librairie Droz S.A., 1970), 65–66: On m'avait contraint de me placer à genoux près de ce lugubre appareil. Tout à coup un murmure confus sort de dessous le voile sépulcral; je m'incline, et ces paroles épouvantables (que je fus seul à entendre) viennent frapper mon oreille: "Dieu de miséricorde, fais que ne me relève jamais de cette couche funèbre, et comble de tes biens un frère qui n'a point partagé ma criminelle passion!"

3. C'est dans les bois de Combourg que je suis devenu ce que je suis... (MOT, livre 3, chapitre 16, 85.)

4. Les patriciens commencèrent la Révolution, les plébéiens l'achevèrent... (MOT, livre 5, chapitre 10, 129.)

5. Dans une société qui se dissout et se recompose....Le genre humain en vacances se promène dans la rue, débarrassé de ses pédagogues rentrés pour un moment dans l'état de nature... (MOT, livre 5, chapitre 14, 136.)

6. Ces têtes, et d'autres que je rencontrai bientôt après, changèrent mes dispositions politiques; j'eus horreur des festins

de cannibales et l'idée de quitter la France pour quelque pays lointain germa dans mon esprit. (MOT, livre 5, chapitre 9, 128.)

7. Gilbert Chinard, *Souvenirs D'Edouard de Mondesir* (Baltimore: Johns Hopkins Press, 1942), 21: M. de Chateaubriand… comme Ulysse, attacher au mât du milieu, oú il fut couvert des vagues de la mer et bien battu du vent. Mais bravant l'air et l'eau, il s'encourageait en criant, "O tempête, tu n'es pas encore si belle qu'Homère t'a faite!"

8. …et pour éviter une tracasserie d'une heure, je me rendrais esclave pendant un siècle. (MOT, livre 9, chapitre 1, 206.)

9. De toutes les peines que j'avais endurées, celle-là me fut la plus sensible et la plus grande. Je me jetai aux genoux de madame Ives; je couvris ses mains de mes baisers et de mes larmes. Elle croyait que je pleurais de bonheur, et elle se mit à sangloter de joie… : "Arrêtez ! m'écriai-je; je suis marié!" Elle tomba évanouie. (MOT, livre 10, chapitre 9, 261.)

10. Irving Putter, *Chateaubriand: Atala/René—A New Translation* (Berkeley: University of California Press, 1952), 6.

11. George Ticknor, *Life, Letters and Journals of George Ticknor* (Boston: J.R. Osgood and Company, 1876), 137.

12. Ibid.

13. Je fus tiré de mes réflexions par le gazouillement d'une grive perchée sur la plus haute branche d'un bouleau. A l'instant, ce son magique fit reparaître à mes yeux le domaine paternel….Le chant de l'oiseau dans les bois de Combourg m'entretenait d'une félicité que je croyais atteindre; le même chant dans le parc de Montboissier me rappelait des jours perdus à la poursuite de cette félicité insaisissable. Je n'ai plus rien à apprendre….Mettons à profit le peu d'instants qui me restent; hâtons-nous de peindre ma jeunesse, tandis que j'y touche encore: le navigateur, abandonnant pour jamais un rivage enchanté, écrit son journal à la vue de la terre qui s'éloigne et qui va bientôt disparaître. (MOT, livre 3, chapitre 1, 65.)

14. Un grand écrivain français
A voulu reposer ici
Pour n'y entendre
Que la mer et le vent
Passant
Respecte sa dernière volonté.
15. Friedrich Sieburg, *Chateaubriand* (London: George Allen & Unwin, 1961), 23.

Chapter 3

1. Paris, le 28 Juin 1817.

Je vous envoye, mon petit ami, un paquet contenant:
un habit bleu
deux pantalons de drap
une culotte noire
une culotte de nankin
deux gilets de piqué blanc

Il faudra que ce effet soyent refaits a votre taille. J'ai envoyé pour cela à M. le Proviseur la somme de 30 f pour en payer la façon. Je lui ai aussi adressé une notice de ce que je vous envoye.

Continuez toujours vos études, mon cher fallon, et comptez sur mon amitié.

deCh

2. Ce n'est que ce matin, Monsieur, que j'ai appris que M. le Viscomte de Chateaubriand vous accordait la permission qu je lui ai demandée pour vous d'aller passer les vacances chez les parents de deux de vos camarades. J'espère qu'il est encore temps de profiter de cette permission. Je suis fâché de n'avoir pu vous annoncer plus tôt. Je vous souhaite toutes sortes d'amusements.

J'ai l'honneur d'être, Monsieur, votre très humble et très obéissant serviteur

Hyacinthe Pilorge

Paris, le 20 aoùt 1817

P.S. Pour que cela ne souffre aucune difficulté, je fais part de cette permission par le même courrier à M. le Proviseur du Collège.

3. Joan Evans, *Chateaubriand: A Biography* (London: Macmillan & Co., 1939), 123–124.

4. Evans, 260.

5. For a review of Chateaubriand's feminine friends, see Jacques Georgel, *Chateaubriand, Dix neuf Femmes et un Fils Américain* (Paris: Editions Le Manuscrit, 2004).

6. …je quittai d'abord Holborn–Tottenham–Courtroad et m'avançai jusque sur la route d'Hampstead. Là, je stationnai quelques mois chez madame O'Larry, veuve irlandaise.…Chez madame O'Larry venaient de vieilles voisines avec lesquelles j'étais obligé de prendre du thé à l'ancienne façon. Madame de Staël a peint cette scène dans Corinne chez lady Edgermond: "Ma chère, croyez-vous que l'eau soit assez bouillante pour la jeter sur le thé? –Ma chère, je crois que ce serait trop tôt." Venait aussi à ces soirées une grande belle jeune Irlandaise, Marie Neale, sous la garde d'un tuteur. Elle trouvait au fond de mon regard quelque blessure, car elle me disait: *You carry your heart in a sling* (vous portez votre cœur en écharpe). Je portais mon cœur je ne sais comment. (MOT, livre 11, chapitre 2, 269–270.) *Note:* In an orthographic error, Chateaubriand spelled "O'Leary" as "O'Larry"; subsequent research has determined that her name was O'Leary. He also used the French spelling "Marie" rather than the English spelling "Mary."

7. Faramerz Dabhoiwala, *The Origins of Sex: A History of the First Sexual Revolution* (Oxford: Oxford University Press, 2012).

8. For a review of sexual mores in England in the seventeenth and eighteenth centuries, along with demographic consequences,

see Edward AnthonyWrigley, "Marriage, Fertility, and Population Growth in Eighteenth Century England," in *Marriage and Society: Studies in the Social History of Marriage*, ed. R. B. Outhwaite (New York: St. Martin's Press, 1982), 137–185.

9. Maurice Levaillant, *Splendeurs Misères et Chimères de Monsieur de Chateaubriand d'après des Documents Inédits* (Paris: Albin Michel, 1948), 108: J'ai toujours oublié de vous demander si vous aviez reçu la quittance du proviseur du lycée d'Amiens. Si vous ne l'avez pas reçue, demandez-la; et dites en même temps que je veux bien que le jeune homme aille passer les vacances chez un de ses camarades.

10. Mes amis…m'installèrent aux environs de Mary-Le-Bone-Street dans un *garret* dont la lucarne donnait sur un cimetière: chaque nuit la crécelle du *watchman* m'annonçait que l'on venait de voler des cadavres. (MOT, Livre 10, chapitre 6, 254.)

11. George D. Painter, "London Garrets," *Adam International Review* 44 (1982): 13–14.

12. Je dirigeais alors ma course à Kensington ou à Westminster. Kensington me plaisait; j'errais dans sa partie solitaire, tandis que la partie qui touchait à Hyde-Park se couvrait d'une multitude brillante. Le contraste de mon indigence et de la richesse, de mon délaissement et de la foule, m'était agréable. (MOT, livre 10, chapitre 5, 250.)

13. Je voyais passer de loin les jeunes Anglaises avec cette confusion désireuse que me faisait éprouver autrefois ma sylphide, lorsqu'après l'avoir parée de toutes mes folies, j'osais à peine lever les yeux sur mon ouvrage. La mort, à laquelle je croyais toucher, ajoutait un mystère à cette vision d'un monde dont j'étais presque sorti. S'est-il jamais attaché un regard sur l'étranger assis au pied d'un pin? Quelque belle femme avait-elle deviné l'invisible présence de René? (MOT, livre 10, chapitre 5, 250.)

14. François-René de Chateaubriand, *The Memoirs of Chateaubriand, Volume II,* trans. Alexander Teixeira de Matos (New York: G.P. Putnam's Sons, 1902), 99.

15. Chateaubriand, *Memoirs from Beyond the Grave,* 466.

Chapter 4

1. Levaillant, 109: Le jeune Fallon paraît n'être demeuré qu'un an à Amiens; les palmarès ne citent pas son nom. On aimerait savoir quel lien précis attache Chateaubriand à ce lycéen, qui a dix-sept à dix huit ans en 1817, juste dix-sept ans après que Chateaubriand est revenu d'Angleterre....Son illustre protecteur continua-t-il de lui marquer de la solicitude? Et que devint-il?

Chapter 5

1. Levaillant, 108: Il vous surviendra encore une pauvre Anglais appellée Mme Fallon. Donnez-lui 100 francs, je vous prie...

2. Pierre Riberette, "La Lettre à Charlotte Ives," *Société Chateaubriand; Bulletin Année* 39 (1997): 16: Sur la recommandation d'un de ses compatriotes lui aussi émigré, le journaliste Peltier, il a trouvé un emploi, plutôt précaire à la vérité, de professeur de français et peut être aussi de maître à danser, attaché à une école de la petite ville de Beccles, dans le Suffolk, tout en donnant des leçons particulières à des jeunes gens du voisinage. Mais n'allez pas croire qu'il aille révéler cette occupation, certes mercenaire, mais tout à fait honorable, dans les *Mémoires d'outre-tombe.* Non! ayant toujours présent à l'esprit la mise en garde d'un de ses parents, le vieil abbé de Chateaubriand de La Guérande, qui déclarait que les Chateaubriand ont pu avoir des précepteurs, mais qu'ils n'ont été les précepteurs de personne, il préfère raconter qu'il a été chargé, par une société savante de l'endroit, qui n'a que le tort de n'avoir jamais existé, de faire des recherches dans une collection

de manuscrits dont personne n'a jamais entendu parler, parce qu'elle est le fruit de son imagination.

3.. Peu à peu, j'éprouvai le charme timide d'un attachement sorti de l'âme... (MOT, livre 10, chapitre 9, 260.)

4. Riberette, 18.

5. ...mon valet de chambre est venu me dire, un matin entre midi et une heure, qu'une voiture était arrêtée à ma porte, et qu'une dame anglaise demandait à me parler. Comme je me suis fait une règle, dans ma position publique, de ne refuser personne, j'ai dit de laisser monter cette dame. J'étais dans mon cabinet; on a annoncé lady Sutton; j'ai vu entrer une femme en deuil, accompagnée de deux beaux garçons également en deuil: l'un pouvait avoir seize ans et l'autre quatorze. Je me suis avancé vers l'étrangère; elle était si émue qu'elle pouvait à peine marcher. Elle m'a dit d'une voix altérée: "My lord, do you remember me? Me reconnaissez-vous?" Oui, j'ai reconnu miss Ives! les années qui avaient passé sur sa tête ne lui avaient laissé que leur printemps. Je l'ai prise par la main, je l'ai fait asseoir et je me suis assis à ses côtés. Je ne lui pouvais parler; mes yeux étaient pleins de larmes; je la regardais en silence à travers ces larmes; je sentais que je l'avais profondément aimée par ce que j'éprouvais. Enfin, j'ai pu lui dire à mon tour: "Et vous, madame, me reconnaissez-vous?" Elle a levé les yeux qu'elle tenait baissés, et, pour toute réponse elle m'a adressé un regard souriant et mélancolique comme un long souvenir. Sa main était toujours entre les deux miennes. Charlotte m'a dit: "Je suis en deuil de ma mère; mon père est mort depuis plusieurs années. Voilà mes enfants." A ces derniers mots, elle a retiré sa main et s'est enfoncée dans son fauteuil, en couvrant ses yeux de son mouchoir. (MOT, livre 10, chapitre 11, 264.)

6. For a discussion of the letter and its significance, see Riberette, 16–21.

7. Fallon, *A Variety of Fallon*, 49.

8. Tim Fanning, *Paisanos: The Forgotten Irish Who Changed the Face of Latin America* (Dublin: Gil Books, 2016).

9. Matthew Brown, *Adventuring through Spanish Colonies: Simón Bolívar, Foreign Mercenaries and the Birth of New Nations* (Liverpool: Liverpool University Press, 2006), 27.

About the Author

Daniel Fallon holds a BA in psychology from Antioch College and an MA and PhD in experimental psychology from the University of Virginia. He is professor emeritus of psychology and professor emeritus of public policy at the University of Maryland at College Park, where he also served as academic vice president and provost. A former adviser and evaluator for the German government on higher education initiatives, he was elected to the board of trustees of two German universities. He concluded his professional career as chair of the Education Division at Carnegie Corporation of New York, where he directed grantmaking in education, focusing principally on adolescent literacy, urban school reform, teacher education reform, and liberal education. He now works as a higher education consultant.

Fallon has published widely on learning, motivation, educational reform, and contemporary cultural issues. He is the author of *The German University: A Heroic Ideal in Conflict with the Modern World*, which was awarded the Eugene M. Kayden prize for excellence in humanities. He has also published program notes for music performances and offered pre-concert lectures. *Love's Legacy*, his latest published work, reflects his decades-long exploration of French literary and cultural history.

Born in Cartagena, Colombia, where his father was then chief of staff of the Colombian Navy, Fallon came to the United States with his parents at two years of age. His mother was a native of New Orleans. He currently lives in Santa Fe, New Mexico.